After Deschooling, What?

After Deschooling, What?

IVAN ILLICH ARTHUR PEARL
HERBERT GINTIS ROY P. FAIRFIELD
COLIN GREER MAXINE GREENE
SUMNER M. ROSEN NEIL POSTMAN
JUDSON JEROME RONALD GROSS

EDITED BY ALAN GARTNER,
COLIN GREER, AND FRANK RIESSMAN

PERENNIAL LIBRARY
Harper & Row, Publishers
New York, Evanston, San Francisco, London

All of these essays appeared in *Social Policy* with the
exception of Herbert Gintis's "Toward a Political
Economy of Education: A Radical Critique of Ivan
Illich's *Deschooling Society*," and "All Schooled Up" by
Colin Greer. Herbert Gintis, "Toward a Political Econ-
omy of Education: A Radical Critique of Ivan Illich's
Deschooling Society," *Harvard Educational Review*, 42,
February 1972, 70–96. Copyright © 1972 by President
and Fellows of Harvard College. Used with permission.
Colin Greer, "All Schooled Up," first appeared in *Sat-
urday Review*, October 16, 1971. Copyright © 1971 by
Saturday Review, Inc. Used with permission.

*A hardcover edition is available from Harper & Row,
Publishers.*

First PERENNIAL LIBRARY edition published 1973.

LIBRARY OF CONGRESS CATALOG CARD NUMBER: 72–11590

STANDARD BOOK NUMBER: 06–080282–0 (PAPERBACK)

STANDARD BOOK NUMBER: 06–136126–7 (HARDCOVER)

ISSUES OF *Social Policy* THAT ESSAYS
APPEARED IN:

IVAN ILLICH/After Deschooling, What?
September–October 1971

NEIL POSTMAN/My Illich Problem
January–February 1972

RONALD GROSS/After Deschooling, Free Learning
January–February 1972

ROY P. FAIRFIELD/Need for a Risk Quotient
January–February 1972

SUMNER M. ROSEN/Taking Illich Seriously
March–April 1972

JUDSON JEROME/After Illich, What?
March–April 1972

MAXINE GREENE/And It Still Is News
March–April 1972

ARTHUR PEARL/The Case for Schooling America
March–April 1972

Contents

Preface

Social Policy published an article by Ivan Illich which went just a little further than his book, *Deschooling Society*. He went beyond his argument for deschooling, to the beginning of some thoughts about what society and education might look like following it.

We then asked a number of serious and active educators to react to the Illich article. They each found the concept of deschooling useful as a framework for summarizing the problems of traditional education. But they differed on the degree to which Illich was useful and/or sensible outside the context of his critique.

Together, all of these articles—Illich himself and the various critiques published in *Social Policy*—provide a stimulating and provocative discussion of some of the basic educational issues raised by the catch-phrase "deschooling." So we thought it a good idea to make the collection available to a larger audience in this first *Social Policy* book.

We have added two articles from other publications: from *Saturday Review* and the *Harvard Educational Review*. We believe that both Colin Greer and Herbert Gintis, in their respective reviews of Ivan Illich's book, *Deschooling Society*, significantly contribute to the range and depth of the critique presented here.

Ivan Illich has become a popular landmark in the American national debate on public education. Since education has itself become so crucial to and reflective of American culture and American social problems, we believe that an understanding of what Illich has to say about education and society is of the utmost importance.

After Deschooling, What?

After Deschooling, What?

IVAN ILLICH

Schools are in crisis, and so are the people who
attend them. The former is a crisis in a political
institution; the latter is a crisis of political attitudes. This second crisis, the crisis of personal
growth, can be dealt with only if understood as
distinct from, though related to, the crisis of the
school.

Schools have lost their unquestioned claim to
educational legitimacy. Most of their critics still
demand a painful and radical reform of the
school, but a quickly expanding minority will not
stand for anything short of the prohibition of
compulsory attendance and the disqualification of
academic certificates. Controversy between partisans of renewal and partisans of disestablishment
will soon come to a head.

As attention focuses on the school, however, we
can be easily distracted from a much deeper concern: the manner in which learning is to be
viewed. Will people continue to treat learning as
a commodity—a commodity that could be more
efficiently produced and consumed by greater numbers of people if new institutional arrangements

were established? Or shall we set up only those institutional arrangements that protect the autonomy of the learner—his private initiative to decide what he will learn and his inalienable right to learn what he likes rather than what is useful to somebody else? We must choose between more efficient education of people fit for an increasingly efficient society and a new society in which education ceases to be the task of some special agency.

Schools Reproduce Society

All over the world schools are organized enterprises designed to reproduce the established order, whether this order is called revolutionary, conservative, or evolutionary. Everywhere the loss of pedagogical credibility and the resistance to schools provide a fundamental option: shall this crisis be dealt with as a problem that can, and must, be solved by substituting new devices for school and readjusting the existing power structure to fit these devices? Or shall this crisis force a society to face the structural contradictions inherent in the politics and economics of any society that reproduces itself through the industrial process?

In the United States and Canada huge investments in schooling only serve to make institutional contradictions more evident. Experts warn us: Charles Silberman's report to the Carnegie Commission, published as *Crisis in the Classroom*, has become a best seller. It appeals to a large public because of its well-documented indictment of the system—in the light of which his attempts to save the school by patching up its most obvious faults pall into insignificance. The Wright Commission, in Ontario, had to report to its government sponsors that postsecondary education is inevitably and without remedy taxing the poor disproportionately for an education that will always be enjoyed mainly by the rich. Experience confirms these warnings: Students and teachers drop out; free schools come and go. Political control of schools replaces bond issues on the platforms of school board candidates, and—as recently happened in Berkeley—advocates of grassroots control are elected to the board.

On March 8, 1971, Chief Justice Warren E. Burger delivered the unanimous opinion of the court in the case of *Griggs v. Duke Power Co.* Interpreting the intent of Congress in the equal opportunities section of the 1964 Civil Rights Act, the Burger Court ruled that any school degree or any test given prospective employees must "measure the man for the job," not "the man in the abstract." The burden for proving that educational requirements are a "reasonable measure of job performance" rests with the employer. In this decision, the court ruled only on the use of tests and diplomas as means of racial discrimination, but the logic of the Chief Justice's argument applies to any use of an educational pedigree as a prerequisite for employment. "The Great Training Robbery" so effectively exposed by Ivar Berg must now face challenge from congeries of pupils, employers, and taxpayers.

In poor countries schools rationalize economic lag. The majority of citizens are excluded from the scarce modern means of production and consumption, but long to enter the economy by way of the school door. And the liberal institution of compulsory schooling permits the well-schooled to impute to the lagging consumer of knowledge the guilt for holding a certificate of lower denomination, thereby rationalizing through a rhetorical populism that is becoming increasingly hard to square with the facts.

Upon seizing power, the military junta in Peru immediately decided to suspend further expenditures on free public school. They reasoned that since a third of the public budget could not provide one full year of decent schooling for all, the available tax receipts could better be spent on a type of educational resources that make them more nearly accessible to all citizens. The educational reform commission appointed by the junta could not fully carry out this decision because of pressures from the school teachers of the APRA, the Communists, and the Cardinal Archbishop of Lima. Now there will be two competing systems of public education in a country that cannot afford one. The resulting contradictions will confirm the original judgment of the junta.

For ten years Castro's Cuba has devoted great energies to rapid-growth popular education, relying on available manpower, without the usual respect for professional credentials. The initial spectacular successes of this campaign, especially in diminishing illiteracy, have been cited as evidence for the claim that the slow growth rate of other Latin American school systems is due to corruption, militarism, and a capitalist market economy. Yet, now, the hidden curriculum of hierarchical schooling is catching up with Fidel and his attempt to school-produce the New Man. Even when students spend half the year in the cane fields and fully subscribe to "fidelismo," the school trains every year a crop of knowledge consumers ready to move on to new levels of consumption. Also, Dr. Castro faces evidence that the school system will never turn out enough certified technical manpower. Those licensed graduates who do get the new jobs destroy, by their conservatism, the results obtained by noncertified cadres who muddled into their positions through on-the-job training. Teachers just cannot be blamed for the failures of a revolutionary government that insists on the institutional capitalization of manpower through a hidden curriculum guaranteed to produce a universal bourgeoisie.

This crisis is epochal. We are witnessing the end of the age of schooling. School has lost the power, which reigned supreme during the first half of this century, to blind its participants to the divergence between the egalitarian myth its rhetoric serves and the rationalization of a stratified society its certificates produce. The loss of legitimacy of the schooling process as a means of determining competence, as a measure of social value, and as an agent of equality threatens all political systems that rely on schools as the means of reproducing themselves.

School is the initiation ritual to a society oriented toward the progressive consumption of increasingly less tangible and more expensive services, a society that relies on worldwide standards, large-scale and long-term planning, constant obsolescence through the built-in ethos of never-ending improvements: the constant translation of new needs into specific demands for the consumption of new satisfactions. This society is proving itself unworkable.

Superficial Solutions

Since the crisis in schooling is symptomatic of a deeper crisis of modern industrial society, it is important that the critics of schooling avoid superficial solutions. Inadequate analysis of the nature of schooling only postpones the facing of deeper issues. But most criticism of the schools is pedagogical, political, or technological. The criticism of the educator is leveled at what is taught and how it is taught. The curriculum is outdated, so we have courses on African culture, on North American imperialism, on Women's Liberation, on food and nutrition. Passive learning is old-fashioned, so we have increased student participation, both in the classroom and in the planning of curriculum. School buildings are ugly, so we have new learning environments. There is concern for the development of human sensitivity, so group threapy methods are imported into the classroom.

Another important set of critics is involved with the politics of urban school administration. They feel that the poor could run their schools better than a centralized bureaucracy that is oblivious to the problems of the dispossessed. Black parents are enlisted to replace white teachers in the motivation of their children to make time and find the will to learn.

Still other critics emphasize that schools make inefficient use of modern technology. They would either electrify the classroom or replace schools with computerized learning centers. If they follow McLuhan, they would replace blackboards and textbooks with multimedia happenings; if they follow Skinner, they would compete with the classical teacher and sell economy packages of measurable behavioral modifications to cost-conscious school boards.

I believe all these critics miss the point, because they fail to attend to what I have elsewhere called the ritual aspects of schooling—what I here propose to call the "hidden curriculum," the structure underlying what has been called the certification effect. Others have used this phrase to refer to the environmental curriculum of the ghetto street or the suburban lawn, which the teacher's curriculum either reinforces or vainly attempts to replace. I am using the term "hidden curriculum" to refer to the structure of schooling as opposed to what happens in school, in the same way that linguists distinguish between the structure of a language and the use the speaker makes of it.

The Real Hidden Curriculum

The traditional hidden curriculum of school demands that people of a certain age assemble in groups of about thirty under the authority of a professional teacher for from five hundred to a thousand times a year. It does not matter if the teacher is authoritarian so long as it is the teacher's authority that counts; it does not matter if all meetings occur in the same place so long as they are somehow understood as attendance. The hidden curriculum of school requires—whether by law or by fact—that a citizen accumulate a minimum quantum of school years in order to obtain his civil rights.

The hidden curriculum of school has been legislated in all the united nations from Afghanistan to Zambia. It is common to the United States and the Soviet Union, to rich nations and poor, to electoral and dictatorial regimes. Whatever the ideologies and techniques explicitly transmitted in their school systems, all these nations assume that political and economic development depend on further investment in schooling.

The hidden curriculum teaches all children that

economically valuable knowledge is the result of professional teaching and that social entitlements depend on the rank achieved in a bureaucratic process. The hidden curriculum transforms the explicit curriculum into a commodity and makes its acquisition the securest form of wealth. Knowledge certificates—unlike property rights, corporate stock, or family inheritance—are free from challenge. They withstand sudden changes of fortune. They convert into guaranteed privilege. That high accumulation of knowledge should convert to high personal consumption might be challenged in North Vietnam or Cuba, but school is universally accepted as the avenue to greater power, to increased legitimacy as a producer, and to further learning resources.

For all its vices, school cannot be simply and rashly eliminated; in the present situation it performs certain important negative functions The hidden curriculum, unconsciously accepted by the liberal pedagogue, frustrates his conscious liberal aims, because it is inherently inconsistent with them. But, on the other hand, it also prevents the take-over of education by the programmed instruction of behavioral technologists. While the hidden curriculum makes social role depend on the process of acquiring knowledge, thus legitimizing stratification, it also ties the learning process to full-time attendance, thus illegitimizing the educational entrepreneur. If the school continues to lose its educational and political legitimacy, while knowledge is still conceived as a commodity, we will certainly face the emergence of a therapeutic Big Brother.

The translation of the need for learning into the demand for schooling and the conversion of the quality of growing up into the price tag of a professional treatment changes the meaning of "knowledge" from a term that designates intimacy, intercourse, and life experience into one that designates professionally packaged products, marketable entitlements, and abstract values. Schools have helped to foster this translation.

Of course schools are by no means the only institutions that pretend to translate knowledge, understanding, and wisdom into behavioral traits, the measurement of which is the key to prestige and power. Nor are schools the first institution used to convert knowledge to power. But it is in large measure the public school that has parlayed the consumption of knowledge into the exercise of privilege and power in a society in which this function coincided with the legitimate aspirations of those members of the lower middle classes for whom schools provided access to the professions.

Expanding the Concept of Alienation

Since the nineteenth century, we have become accustomed to the claim that man in a capitalist economy is alienated from his labor, that he cannot enjoy it, and that he is deprived of its fruits by those who own the tools of production. Most

countries that officially subscribe to Marxist ideology have had only limited success in changing
this exploitation, and then usually by shifting its
benefits from the owners to the New Class and
from the living generation to the members of the
future nation-state.

The concept of alienation cannot help us understand the present crisis unless it is applied not
only to the purposeful and productive use of human endeavor but also to the use made of men as
the recipients of professional treatments. An ex-
panded understanding of alienation would enable
us to see that in a service-centered economy man
is estranged from what he can "do" as well as from
what he can "make," that he has delivered his
mind and heart over to therapeutic treatment even
more completely than he has sold the fruits of his
labor.

Schools have alienated man from his learning.
He does not enjoy going to school. If he is poor,
he does not get the reputed benefits; if he does all
that is asked of him, he finds his security constantly
threatened by more recent graduates; if he is sensitive, he feels deep conflicts between what is and
what is supposed to be. He does not trust his own
judgment, and even if he resents the judgment of
the educator, he is condemned to accept it and to
believe that he cannot change reality. The converging crisis of ritual schooling and of acquisitive
knowledge raises the deeper issue of the tolerability
of life in an alienated society. If we formulate
principles for alternative institutional arrange-

ments and an alternative emphasis in the conception of learning, we will also be suggesting principles for a radically alternative political and economic organization.

Just as the structure of one's native language can be grasped only after he has begun to feel at ease in another tongue, so the fact that the hidden curriculum of schooling has moved out of the blind spot of social analysis indicates that alternative forms of social initiation are beginning to emerge and are permitting some of us to see things from a new perspective. Today it is relatively easy to get wide agreement on the fact that gratuitous, compulsory schooling is contrary to the political self-interest of an enlightened majority. School has become pedagogically indefensible as an instrument of universal education. It no longer even fits the needs of the seductive salesman of programmed learning. Proponents of recorded, filmed, and computerized instruction used to court the schoolmen as business prospects; now they are itching to do the job on their own.

As more and more sectors of society become dissatisfied with school and conscious of its hidden curriculum, increasingly large concessions are made to translate their demands into needs that can be served by the system—and thus disarm their dissent. As the hidden curriculum moves out of the darkness and into the twilight of our awareness, phrases such as the "deschooling of society" and the "disestablishment of schools" become instant slogans. I do not think these phrases were used before last year. This year they have become, in some circles, the badge and criterion of the new orthodoxy. Recently I talked by amplified telephone to students in a seminar on deschooling at the Ohio State University College of Education. Everett Reimer's book on deschooling became a popular college text even before it was commercially published. But this is urgently important: Unless the radical critics of school are not only ready to embrace the deschooling slogan but also prepared to reject the current view that learning and growing up can be adequately explained as a process of programming, and the current vision of social justice based on it—more obligatory consumption for everybody—we may face the charge of having provoked the last of the missed revolutions.

Schools Are Too Easy Targets

The current crisis has made it easy to attack schools. Schools, after all, are authoritarian and rigid; they do produce both conformity and conflict; they do discriminate against the poor and disengage the privileged. These are not new facts, but it used to be a mark of some boldness to point them out. Now it takes a good deal of courage to defend schools. It has become fashionable to poke fun at alma mater, to take a potshot at the former sacred cow.

Once the vulnerability of schools has been exposed, it becomes easy to suggest remedies for the most outrageous abuses. The authoritarian rule of the classroom is not intrinsic to the notion of an extended confinement of children in schools. Free schools are practical alternatives; they can often be run more cheaply than ordinary schools. Since accountability already belongs to educational rhetoric, community control and performance contracting have become attractive and respectable political goals. Everyone wants education to be relevant to real life, so critics talk freely about pushing back the classroom walls to the borders of our culture. Not only are alternatives more widely advocated, they are often at least partially implemented: experimental schools are financed by school boards; the hiring of certified teachers is decentralized; high school credit is given for apprenticeship and college credit, for travel; computer games are given a trial run.

Most of the changes have some good effects: the experimental schools have fewer truants; parents have a greater feeling of participation in the decentralized districts; children who have been introduced to real jobs do turn out more competent. Yet all these alternatives operate within predictable limits, since they leave the hidden structure of schools intact. Free schools, which lead to further free schools in an unbroken chain of attendance, produce the mirage of freedom. Attendance as the result of seduction inculcates the need for specialized treatment more persuasively than reluctant attendance enforced by truant officers. Free school graduates are easily rendered impotent for life in a society that bears little resemblance to the protected gardens in which they have been cultivated. Community control of the lower levels of a system turns local school board members into pimps for the professional hookers who control the upper levels. Learning by doing is not worth much if doing has to be defined, by professional educators or by law, as socially valuable learning. The global village will be a global schoolhouse if teachers hold all the strings. It would be distinguishable in name only from a global madhouse run by social therapists or a global prison run by corporation wardens.

In a general way I have pointed out the dangers of a rash, uncritical disestablishment of school. More concretely, these dangers are exemplified by various kinds of co-option that change the hidden curriculum without changing the basic concepts of learning and of knowledge and their relationship to the freedom of the individual in society.

Benign Inequality

The rash and uncritical disestablishment of school could lead to a free-for-all in the production and consumption of more vulgar learning, acquired for immediate utility or eventual prestige. The discrediting of school-produced, complex, curricular packages would be an empty victory if there were no simultaneous disavowal of the very idea that knowledge is more valuable because it comes in certified packages and is acquired from some mythological knowledge-stock controlled by professional guardians. I believe that only actual participation constitutes socially valuable learning, a participation by the learner in every stage of the learning process, including not only a free choice of what is to be learned and how it is to be learned but also a free determination by each learner of his own reason for living and learning —the part that his knowledge is to play in his life.

Social control in an apparently deschooled society could be more subtle and more numbing than in the present society, in which many people at least experience a feeling of release on the last day of school. More intimate forms of manipulation are already common, as the amount learned through the media exceeds the amount learned through personal contact in and out of school. Learning from programmed information always hides reality behind a screen.

Let me illustrate the paralyzing effects of programmed information by a perhaps shocking example. The tolerance of the American people to United States atrocities in Vietnam is much higher than the tolerance of the German people to German atrocities on the front, in occupied territories, and in extermination camps during World War II. It was a political crime for Germans to discuss the atrocities committed by Germans. The presentation of U.S. atrocities on network television is considered an educational service. Certainly the population of the United States is much better informed about the crimes committed by its troops in a colonial war than were the Germans about the crimes committed by its SS within the territory of the Reich. To get information on atrocities in Germany meant that one had to take a great risk; in the United States the same information is channeled into one's living room. This does not mean, however, that the Germans were any less aware that their government was engaged in cruel and massive crime than are contemporary Americans. In fact, it can be argued that the Germans were *more* aware precisely because they were not psychically overwhelmed with packaged information about killing and torture, because they were not drugged into accepting that everything is possible, because they were not vaccinated against reality by having it fed to them as decomposed "bits" on a screen.

The consumer of precooked knowledge learns to react to knowledge he has acquired rather than to the reality from which a team of experts has abstracted it. If access to reality is always controlled by a therapist and if the learner accepts this control as natural, his entire worldview becomes hygienic and neutral; he becomes politically impotent. He becomes impotent to know in the sense of the Hebrew word *jdh*, which means intercourse penetrating the nakedness of being and reality, because the reality for which he can accept responsibility is hidden from him under the scales of assorted information he has accumulated.

The uncritical disestablishment of school could also lead to new performance criteria for preferential employment and promotion and, most importantly, for privileged access to tools. Our present scale of "general" ability, competence, and trustworthiness for role assignment is calibrated by tolerance to high doses of schooling. It is established by teachers and accepted by many as rational and benevolent. New devices could be developed, and new rationales found, both more insidious than school grading and equally effective in justifying social stratification and the accumulation of privilege and power.

Participation in military, bureaucratic, or political activities or status in a party could provide a pedigree just as transferable to other institutions as the pedigree of grandparents in an aristocratic society, standing within the Church in medieval society, or age at graduation in a schooled society. General tests of attitudes, intelligence, or mechanical ability could be standardized according to criteria other than those of the schoolmaster. They could reflect the ideal levels of professional treatment espoused by psychiatrist, ideologue, or bureaucrat. Academic criteria are already suspect. The Center for Urban Studies of Columbia University has shown that there is less correlation between specialized education and job performance in specialized fields than there is between specialized education and the resulting income, prestige, and administrative power. Nonacademic criteria are already proposed. From the urban ghetto in the United States to the villages of China, revolutionary groups try to prove that ideology and militancy are types of "learning" that convert more suitably into political and economic power than scholastic curricula. Unless we guarantee that job relevance is the only acceptable criterion for employment, promotion, or access to tools, thus ruling out not only schools but all other ritual screening, then deschooling means driving out the devil with Beelzebub.

The Need for Political Objectives

The search for a radical alternative to the school system itself will be of little avail unless it finds expression in precise political demands: the demand for the disestablishment of school in the broadest sense and the correlative guarantee of freedom for education. This means legal protections, a political program, and principles for the construction of institutional arrangements that are the inverse of school. Schools cannot be disestablished without the total prohibition of legislated attendance, the proscription of any discrimination on the basis of prior attendance, and the transfer of control over tax funds from benevolent institutions to the individual person. Even these actions, however, do not guarantee freedom of education unless they are accompanied by positive recognition of each person's independence in the face of school and of any other device designed to compel specific behavioral change or to measure man in the abstract rather than to measure man for a concrete job.

Deschooling makes strange bedfellows. The ambiguity inherent in the breakdown of schooling is manifested by the unholy alliance of groups that can identify their vested interests with the disestablishment of school: students, teachers, employers, opportunistic politicians, taxpayers, Supreme Court justices. But this alliance becomes unholy, and this bedfellowship more than strange, if it is based only on the recognition that schools are inefficient tools for the production and consumption of education and that some other form of mutual exploitation would be more satisfactory.

We can disestablish schools, or we can deschool culture. We can resolve provisionally some of the administrative problems of the knowledge industry, or we can spell out the goals of political revolution in terms of educational postulates. The acid test of our response to the present crisis is our pinpointing of the responsibility for teaching and learning.

Schools have made teachers into administrators of programs of manpower capitalization through directed, planned, behavioral changes. In a schooled society, the ministrations of professional teachers become a first necessity that hooks pupils into unending consumption and dependence. Schools have made "learning" a specialized activity. Deschooling will be only a displacement of responsibility to other kinds of administration so long as teaching and learning remain sacred activities separate and estranged from fulfilling life. If schools were disestablished for the purpose of more efficient delivery of "knowledge" to more people, the alienation of men through client relationships with the new knowledge industry would just become global.

Deschooling must be the secularization of teaching and learning. It must involve a return of control to another, more amorphous set of institutions, and its perhaps less obvious representatives. The learner must be guaranteed his freedom without guaranteeing to society what learning he will acquire and hold as his own. Each man must be guaranteed privacy in learning, with the hope that he will assume the obligation of helping others to grow into uniqueness. Whoever takes the risk of teaching others must assume responsibility for the results, as must the student who exposes himself to the influence of a teacher; neither should shift guilt to sheltering institutions or laws. A schooled society must reassert the joy of conscious living over the capitalization of manpower.

Three Radical Demands

Any dialogue about knowledge is really a dialogue about the individual in society. An analysis of the present crisis of school leads one, then, to talk about the social structure necessary to facilitate learning, to encourage independence and inter-relationship, and to overcome alienation. This kind of discourse is outside the usual range of educational concern. It leads, in fact, to the enun-ciation of specific political goals. These goals can be most sharply defined by distinguishing three general types of "intercourse" in which a person must engage if he would grow up.

Get at the facts, get access to the tools, and bear the responsibility for the limits within which either can be used. If a person is to grow up, he needs, in the first place, access to things, places, processes, events, and records. To guarantee such access is primarily a matter of unlocking the privileged storerooms to which they are presently consigned.

The poor child and the rich child are different partly because what is a secret for one is patent to the other. By turning knowledge into a com-modity, we have learned to deal with it as with private property. The principle of private prop-erty is now used as the major rationale for de-claring certain facts off limits to people without the proper pedigree. The first goal of a political program aimed at rendering the world educational is the abolition of the right to restrict access to teaching or learning. The right of private pre-serve is now claimed by individuals, but it is most effectively exercised and protected by corporations, bureaucracies, and nation-states. In fact, the aboli-tion of this right is not consistent with the continuation of either the political or the professional structure of any modern nation. This means more than merely improving the distribution of teaching materials or providing financial entitlements for the purchase of educational objects. The abolition of secrets clearly transcends conventional proposals for educational reform, yet it is precisely from an educational point of view that the necessity of stating this broad—and perhaps unattainable—political goal is most clearly seen.

The learner also needs access to persons who can teach him the tricks of their trades or the rudiments of their skills. For the interested learner, it does not take much time to learn how to perform most skills or to play most roles. The best teacher of a skill is usually someone who is engaged in its useful exercise. We tend to forget these things in a society in which professional teachers monopolize initiation into all fields and disqualify unauthorized teaching in the community. An important political goal, then, is to provide incentives for the sharing of acquired skills.

The demand that skills be shared implies, of course, a much more radical vision of a desirable future. Access to skills is restricted not just by the monopoly of schools and unions over licensing: there is also the fact that the exercise of skills is tied to the use of scarce tools. Scientific knowledge is overwhelmingly incorporated into tools that are highly specialized and that must be used within complex structures set up for the "efficient" production of goods and services for which demand becomes general while supply remains scarce. Only a privileged few get the results of sophisticated medical research, and only a privileged few get to be doctors. A relatively small minority will travel on supersonic airplanes, and only a few pilots will know how to fly them.

The simplest way to state the alternatives to this trend toward specialization of needs and their satisfaction is in educational terms. It is a question of the desirable use of scientific knowledge. In order to facilitate more equal access to the benefits of science and to decrease alienation and unemployment, we must favor the incorporation of scientific knowledge into tools or components within the reach of a great majority of people.

Insight into the conditions necessary for the wider acquisition and use of skills permits us to define a fundamental characteristic of postindustrial socialism. It is of no use—indeed it is fraudulent—to promote public ownership of the tools of production in an industrial, bureaucratic society. Factories, highways, and heavy-duty trucks can be symbolically "*owned*" by all the people, as the Gross National Product and the Gross National Education are pursued in their name. But the specialized means of producing scarce goods and services cannot be *used* by the majority of people. Only tools that are cheap and simple enough to be accessible and usable by all people, tools that permit temporary association of those who want to use them for a specific occasion, tools that allow specific goals to emerge during their use—only such tools foster the recuperation of work and leisure now alienated through an industrial mode of production.

To recognize, from an educational point of view, the priority of guaranteeing access to tools and components whose simplicity and durability permit their use in a wide variety of creative enterprises is simultaneously to indicate the solution to the problem of unemployment. In an industrial society, unemployment is experienced as the sad inactivity of a man for whom there is nothing to make and who has "unlearned" what to do. Since there is little really useful work, the problem is usually "solved" by creating more jobs in service industries like the military, public administration, education, or social work. Educational considerations oblige me to recommend the substitution of the present mode of industrial production, which depends on a growing market for increasingly complex and obsolescent goods, by a mode of post-industrial production that depends on the demand for tools or components that are labor intensive and repair intensive, and whose complexity is strictly limited.

Science will be kept artificially arcane so long as its results are incorporated into technology at the service of professionals. If it were used to render possible a style of life in which each man could enjoy housing, healing, educating, moving, and entertaining himself, then scientists would try much harder to retranslate the discoveries made in a secret language into the normal language of everyday life.

Self-Evident Educational Freedoms

The level of education in any society can be gauged by the degree of effective access each of the members has to the facts and tools that—within this society—affect his life. We have seen that such access requires a radical denial of the right to secrecy of facts and complexity of tools on which contemporary technocracies found their privilege, which they, in turn, render immune by interpreting its use as a service to the majority. A satisfactory level of education in a technological society imposes important constraints on the use to which scientific knowledge is put. In fact, a technological society that provides conditions for men to recuperate personally (and not institutionally) the sense of potency to learn and to produce, which gives meaning to life, depends on restrictions that must be imposed on the technocrat who now controls both services and manufacture. Only an enlightened and powerful majority can impose such constraints.

If access to facts and use of tools constitute the two most obvious freedoms needed to provide educational opportunity, the ability to convoke peers to a meeting constitutes the one through which the learning by an individual is translated into political process—and political process, in turn, becomes conscious personal growth. Data and skills an individual might have acquired shape into exploratory, creative, open-ended, and personal meaning only when they are used in dialectic encounter. And this requires the guaranteed freedom for every individual to state, each day, the class of issue which he wants to discuss, the class of creative use of a skill in which he seeks a match—to make this bid known—and, within reason, to find the circumstances to meet with peers who join his class. The rights of free speech, free press, and free assembly have traditionally meant this freedom. Modern electronics, photo-offset, and computer techniques in principle have provided the hardware that can provide this freedom with a range undreamt of in the century of enlightenment. Unfortunately, the scientific know-how has been used mainly to increase the power and decrease the number of funnels through which the bureaucrats of education, politics, and information channel their quick-frozen TV dinners. But the same technology could be used to make peer-matching, meeting, and printing as available as the private conversation over the telephone is now.

On the other hand, those who are both dispossessed and disabused of the dream of joy via constantly increasing quanta of consumption need to define what constitutes a desirable society. Only then can the inversion of institutional arrangement here drafted be put into effect—and with it a technological society that values occupation, intensive work, and leisure over alienation through goods and services.

Toward a Political Economy of Education: A Radical Critique of Ivan Illich's *Deschooling Society*

HERBERT GINTIS

Ivan Illich's *Deschooling Society*, despite its bare 115 pages, embraces the world. Its ostensible focus on education moves him inexorably and logically through the panoply of human concerns in advanced industrial society—a society plainly in progressive disintegration and decay. With Yeats we may feel that "things fall apart / The center cannot hold," but Illich's task is no less than to discover and analyze that "center." His endeavor affords the social scientist the unique and rare privilege to put in order the historical movements which characterize our age and define the prospects for a revolutionary future. Such is the subject of this essay.

This little book would have been unthinkable ten years ago. In it, Ivan Illich confronts the full spectrum of the modern crisis in values by reject-

The ideas in this paper were developed in cooperation with Samuel Bowles, whose help in preparing this manuscript was integral.

ing the basic tenets of progressive liberalism. He dismisses what he calls the Myth of Consumption as a cruel and illusory ideology foisted upon the populace by a manipulative bureaucratic system. He treats welfare and service institutions as part of the problem, not as part of the solution. He rejects the belief that education constitutes the "great equalizer" and the path to personal liberation. Schools, say Illich, simply must be eliminated.

Illich does more than merely criticize; he conceptualizes constructive technological alternatives to repressive education. Moreover, he sees the present age as "revolutionary" because the existing social relations of economic and political life, including the dominant institutional structure of schooling, have become impediments to the development of liberating, socially productive technologies. Here Illich is relevant indeed, for the tension between technological possibility and social reality pervades all advanced industrial societies today. Despite our technological power, communities and environment continue to deteriorate, poverty and inequality persist, work remains alienating, and men and women are not liberated for self-fulfilling activity.

Illich's response is a forthright vision of participatory, decentralized, and liberating learning technologies, and a radically altered vision of social relations in education.

Yet, while his *description* of modern society is sufficiently critical, his *analysis* is simplistic and his program, consequently, is a diversion from the immensely complex and demanding political, organizational, intellectual, and personal demands of revolutionary reconstruction in the coming decades. It is crucial that educators and students who have been attracted to him—for his message does correspond to their personal frustration and disillusionment—move beyond him.

The first part of this essay presents Illich's analysis of the economically advanced society—the basis for his analysis of schools. Whereas Illich locates the source of the social problems and value crises of modern societies in their need to reproduce alienated patterns of *consumption,* I argue that these patterns are merely manifestations of the deeper workings of the economic system. The second part of the essay attempts to show that Illich's overemphasis on consumption leads him to a very partial understanding of the functions of the educational system and the contradictions presently besetting it, and hence to ineffective educational alternatives and untenable political strategies for the implementation of desirable educational technologies.

Finally, I argue that a radical theory of educational reform becomes viable only by envisioning liberating and equal education as serving and being served by a radically altered nexus of social relations in *production.* Schools may lead or lag in this process of social transformation, but structural changes in the educational process can be socially relevant only when they speak to potentials for liberation and equality in our day-to-day labors. In the final analysis "de-schooling" is irrelevant because we cannot "de-factory," de-office," or "de-family," save perhaps at the still unenvisioned end of a long process of social reconstruction.

The Social Context of Modern Schooling: Institutionalized Values and Commodity Fetishism

Educational reformers commonly err by treating the system of schools as if it existed in a social vacuum. Illich does not make this mistake. Rather, he views the internal irrationalities of modern education as reflections of the larger society. The key to understanding the problems of advanced industrial economies, he argues, lies in the character of its consumption activities and the ideology which supports them. The schools in turn are exemplary models of bureaucracies geared toward the indoctrination of docile and manipulable consumers.

Guiding modern social life and interpersonal behavior, says Illich, is a destructive system of "institutionalized values" which determine how one perceives one's needs and defines instruments for their satisfaction. The process which creates institutional values insures that all individual needs —physical, psychological, social, intellectual, emotional, and spiritual—are transformed into demands for goods and services. In contrast to the "psychological impotence" which results from in-stitutionalized values, Illich envisages the "psychic health" which emerges from self-realization—both personal and social. Guided by institutionalized values, one's well-being lies not in what one *does* but in what one *has*—the status of one's job and the level of material consumption. For the active person, goods are merely means to or instruments in the performance of activities; for the passive consumer, however, goods are ends in themselves, and activity is merely the means toward sustaining or displaying a desired level of consumption. Thus institutionalized values manifest themselves psy-chologically in a rigorous fetishism—in this case, of commodities and public services. Illich's vision rests in the negation of commodity fetishism:[1]

I believe that a desirable future depends on our de-liberately . . . engendering a life style which will en-able us to be spontaneous, independent, yet related to each other, rather than maintaining a life style which only allows us to make and unmake, produce and con-sume. [*Deschooling Society,* hereafter *DS,* p. 52]

Commodity fetishism is institutionalized in two senses. First, the "delivery systems" in modern in-dustrial economies (i.e., the suppliers of goods and services) are huge, bureaucratic institutions which treat individuals as mere receptors for their products. Goods are supplied by hierarchical and impersonal corporate enterprises, while services

[1] Illich himself does not use the term "commodity fetish-ism." I shall do so, however, as it is more felicitous than "institutionalized values" in many contexts.

are provided by welfare bureaucracies which enjoy ". . . a professional, political and financial
monopoly over the social imagination, setting
standards of what is valuable and what is feasible.
. . . A whole society is initiated into the Myth of
Unending Consumption of services" (DS, p. 44).

Second, commodity fetishism is institutionalized
in the sense that the values of passive consumerism
are induced and reinforced by the same "delivery
systems" whose ministrations are substitutes for
self-initiated activities.

. . . manipulative institutions . . . are either socially
or psychologically "addictive." Social addiction . . .
consists in the tendency to prescribe increased treatment if smaller quantities have not yielded the desired
results. Psychological addiction . . . results when consumers become hooked on the need for more and more
of the process or product. [DS, p. 55]

These delivery systems moreover "both invite com-
pulsively repetitive use and frustrate alternative
ways of achieving similar results." For example,
General Motors and Ford

. . . produce means of transportation, but they also,
and more importantly, manipulate public taste in such
a way that the need for transportation is expressed as
a demand for private cars rather than public buses.
They sell the desire to control a machine, to race at
high speeds in luxurious comfort, while also offering
the fantasy at the end of the road. [DS, p. 57]

This analysis of addictive manipulation in private production is, of course, well-developed in

the literature.[2] Illich's contribution is to extend it to the sphere of service and welfare bureaucracies:

Finally, teachers, doctors, and social workers realize that their distinct professional ministrations have one aspect —at least—in common. They create further demands for the institutional treatments they provide, faster than they can provide service institutions. [*DS*, p. 112]

The well-socialized naturally react to these failures simply by increasing the power and jurisdiction of welfare institutions. Illich's reaction, of course, is precisely the contrary.

The Political Response to Institutionalized Values

As the basis for his educational proposals, Illich's overall framework bears close attention. Since commodity fetishism is basically a psychological stance, it must first be attacked on an individual rather than political level. For Illich, each individual is responsible for his/her own demystification. The institutionalization of values occurs

[2] See, for instance, Herbert Gintis, "Commodity Fetishism and Irrational Production" (Cambridge, Mass.: Harvard Institute for Economic Research, 1970); "Consumer Behavior and the Concept of Sovereignty," *American Economic Review*, forthcoming; "A Radical Analysis of Welfare Economics and Individual Development," *Quarterly Journal of Economics*, forthcoming; John K. Galbraith, *The New Industrial State* (Boston: Houghton Mifflin, 1963); Herbert Marcuse, *One Dimensional Man* (Boston: Beacon Press, 1964).

not through external coercion, but through psychic manipulation, so its rejection is an apolitical act of individual will. The movement for social change thus becomes a cultural one of raising consciousness.

But even on this level, political action in the form of *negating* psychic manipulation is crucial. Goods and services as well as welfare bureaucracies must be *prohibited* from disseminating fetishistic values. Indeed, this is the basis for a political program of deschooling. The educational system, as a coercive source of institutionalized values, must be denied its preferred status. Presumably, this "politics of negation" would extend to advertising and all other types of psychic manipulation.

Since the concrete social manifestation of commodity fetishism is a grossly inflated level of production and consumption, the second step in Illich's political program is the substitution of leisure for work. Work is evil for Illich—unrewarding by its very nature—and not to be granted the status of "activity":

. . . "making and acting" are different, so different, in fact, that one never includes the other. . . . Modern technology has increased the ability of man to relinquish the "making" of things to machines, and his potential time for "acting" has increased. . . . Unemployment is the sad idleness of a man who, contrary to Aristotle, believes that making things, or working, is virtuous and that idleness is bad. [*DS*, p. 62]

Again, Illich's shift in the work-leisure choice is basically apolitical and will follow naturally from the abolition of value indoctrination. People work so hard and long because they are taught to believe the fruits of their activities—consumption—are intrinsically worthy. Elimination of the "hard-sell pitch" of bureaucratic institutions will allow individuals to discover *within themselves* the falsity of the doctrine.

The third stage in Illich's political program envisages the necessity of concrete change in social "delivery systems." Manipulative institutions must be *dismantled,* to be replaced by organizational forms which allow for the free development of individuals. Illich calls such institutions "convivial," and associates them with leftist political orientation.

The regulation of convivial institutions sets limits to their use; as one moves from the convivial to the manipulative end of the spectrum, the rules progressively call for unwilling consumption or participation. . . . Toward, but not at, the left on the institutional spectrum, we can locate enterprises which compete with others in their own field, but have not begun notably to engage in advertising. Here we find hand laundries, small bakeries, hairdressers, and—to speak of professionals—some lawyers and music teachers. . . . They acquire clients through their personal touch and the comparative quality of their services. [*DS,* pp. 55–56]

In short, Illich's Good Society is based on small-scale entrepreneurial (as opposed to corporate) capitalism, with perfectly competitive markets in goods and services. The role of the state in this society is the prevention of manipulative advertising, the development of left-convivial technologies compatible with self-initiating small-group welfare institutions (education, health and medical services, crime prevention and rehabilitation, community development, etc.) and the provisioning of the social infrastructure (e.g., public transportation). Illich's proposal for "learning webs" in education is only a particular application of this vision of left-convivial technologies.

Assessing Illich's Politics: An Overview

Illich's model of consumption-manipulation is crucial at every stage of his political argument. But it is substantially incorrect. In the following three sections I shall criticize three basic thrusts of his analysis.

First, Illich locates the source of social decay in the autonomous, manipulative behavior of corporate bureaucracies. I shall argue, in contrast, that the source must be sought in the normal operation of the basic *economic* institutions of capitalism (markets in factors of production, private control of resources and technology, etc.),[3] which con-

[3] Throughout this paper, I restrict my analysis to *capitalist* as opposed to other economic systems of advanced industrial societies (e.g., state-socialism of the Soviet Union type). As Illich suggests, the *outcomes* are much the same, but the *mechanisms* are in fact quite different. The private-administrative economic power of a capitalist elite is mirrored by the public-administrative political power of a bureaucratic elite in state-socialist countries, and both are used to reproduce a similar complex of social relations of production and a structurally equivalent system of class relations. The capitalist variety is emphasized here because of its special relevance in the American context.

sistently sacrifice the healthy development of community, work, environment, education, and social equality to the accumulation of capital and the growth of marketable goods and services. Moreover, given that individuals must participate in economic activity, these social outcomes are quite insensitive to the preferences or values of individuals, and are certainly in no sense a reflection of the autonomous wills of manipulating bureaucrats or gullible consumers. Hence merely ending "manipulation" while maintaining basic economic institutions will affect the rate of social decay only minimally.

Second, Illich locates the *source* of consumer consciousness in the manipulative socialization of individuals by agencies controlled by corporate and welfare bureaucracies. This "institutionalized consciousness" induces individuals to choose outcomes not in conformity with their "real" needs. I shall argue, in contrast, that a causal analysis can *never* take socialization agencies as basic explanatory variables in assessing the overall behavior of the social system.[4] In particular, consumer consciousness is generated through *the day-to-day activities and observations* of individuals in capitalist society. The sales pitches of manipulative institutions, rather than *generating* the values of commodity fetishism, merely *capitalize* upon and *reinforce* a set of values derived from and reconfirmed by daily personal experience in

[4] Gintis, "Consumer Behavior and the Concept of Sovereignty."

the social system. In fact, while consumer behavior may seem irrational and fetishistic, it is a reasonable accommodation to the options for meaningful social outlets *in the context* of capitalist institutions. Hence the abolition of addictive propaganda cannot "liberate" the individual to "free choice" of personal goals. Such choice is still conditioned by the pattern of social processes which have historically rendered him or her amenable to "institutionalized values." In fact, the likely outcome of demanipulation of values would be no significant alteration of values at all.

Moreover, the ideology of commodity fetishism not only *reflects* the day-to-day operations of the economic system, it is also *functionally necessary* to motivate men/women to accept and participate in the system of alienated production, to peddle their (potentially) creative activities to the highest bidder through the market in labor, to accept the destruction of their communities, and to bear allegiance to an economic system whose market institutions and patterns of control of work and community systematically subordinate all social goals to the criteria of profit and marketable product. Thus the weakening of institutionalized values would in itself lead logically either to unproductive and undirected social chaos (witness the present state of counterculture movements in the United States) or to a rejection of the social relations of capitalist production along with commodity fetishism.

Third, Illich argues that the goal of social

change is to transform institutions according to the criterion of "nonaddictiveness," or "left-conviviality." However, since manipulation and addictiveness are not the sources of social decay, their elimination offers no cure. Certainly the implementation of left-convivial forms in welfare and service agencies—however desirable in itself—will not counter the effects of capitalist development on social life. More important, Illich's criterion explicitly accepts those basic economic institutions which structure decision-making power, lead to the growth of corporate and welfare bureaucracies, and lie at the root of social decay. Thus Illich's criterion must be replaced by one of democratic, participatory, and rationally decentralized control over social outcomes in factory, office, community, schools, and media. The remainder of this essay will elucidate the alternative analysis and political strategy as focused on the particular case of the educational system.

Economic Institutions and Social Development

In line with Illich's suggestion, we may equate individual welfare with the pattern of day-to-day *activities* the individual enters into, together with the personal *capacities*—physical, cognitive, affective, spiritual, and esthetic—he or she has developed toward their execution and appreciation.

Most individual activity is not purely personal, but is based on social interaction and requires a social setting conducive to developing the relevant capacities for performance. That is, activities take place within socially structured domains, characterized by legitimate and socially acceptable roles available to the individual in social relations. The most important of these activity contexts are work, community, and natural environment. The character of individual participation in these contexts —the defining roles one accepts as worker and community member and the way one relates to one's environment—is a basic determinant of well-being and individual development.

These activity contexts, as I shall show, are structured in turn by the way people structure their *productive relations*. The study of activity contexts in capitalist society must begin with an understanding of the basic economic institutions which regulate their historical development.

The most important of these institutions are: (1) *private ownership* of factors of production (land, labor, and capital), according to which the owner has full control over their disposition and development; (2) *a market in labor*, according to which (a) the worker is divorced, by and large, from ownership of nonhuman factors of production (land and capital) (b) the worker relinquishes control over the disposition of his labor during the stipulated workday by exchanging it for money, and (c) the price of a particular type of labor (skilled or unskilled, white collar or blue collar, physical, mental, managerial, or technical) is determined essentially by supply and demand; (3) a *market in land,* according to which the price of each parcel of land is determined by supply and demand, and the use of such parcels is individually determined by the highest bidder; (4) income determination on the basis of the *market-dictated returns to owned factors* of production; (5) *markets in essential commodities*—food, shelter, social insurance, medical care; and (6) *control of the productive process by owners of capital* or their managerial representatives.[5]

Because essential goods, services, and activity contexts are marketed, income is a prerequisite to social existence. Because factors of production are privately owned and market-determined factor returns are the legitimate source of income, and because most workers possess little more than their own labor services, they are required to provide these services to the economic system. Thus control over the developing of work roles and of the social technology of production passes into the hands of the representatives of capital.

Thus the activity context of work becomes alienated in the sense that its structure and historical development do not conform to the needs of the

[5] The arguments in this section are presented at greater length in Gintis, "Power and Alienation," in *Readings in Political Economy,* ed. James Weaver (Rockleigh, N.J.: Allyn and Bacon, 1972) and "Consumer Behavior and the Concept of Sovereignty."

individuals it affects.[6] Bosses determine the technologies and social relations of production within the enterprise on the basis of three criteria. First, production must be flexibly organized for decision-making and secure managerial control from the highest levels downward. This means generally that technologies employed must be compatible with hierarchical authority and a fragmented, task-specific division of labor.[7] The need to maintain effective administrative power leads to bureaucratic order in production, the hallmark of modern corporate organization. Second, among all technologies and work roles compatible with secure and flexible control from the top, bosses choose those which minimize costs and maximize profits. Finally, bosses determine product attributes—and hence the "craft rationality" of production—according to their contribution to gross sales and growth of the enterprise. Hence the decline in pride of workmanship and quality of production associated with the Industrial Revolution.

There is no reason to believe that a great deal of desirable work is not possible. On the contrary, evidence indicates that decentralization, worker control, the reintroduction of craft in production, job rotation, and the elimination of the most con-

[6] This definition conforms to Marxist usage in that "alienation" refers to *social processes*, not psychological states. For some discussion of this term in Marxist literature, see Gintis, "Power and Alienation" and "Consumer Behavior and the Concept of sovereignty."

[7] See the essay by Stephen Marglin, "What Do Bosses Do?" Unpublished, Department of Economics, Harvard University, 1971.

straining aspects of hierarchy are both feasible and potentially efficient. But such work roles develop in an institutional context wherein control, profit, and growth regulate the development of the social relations of production. Unalienated production must be the result of the revolutionary transformation of the basic institutions which Illich implicitly accepts.

The development of communities as activity contexts also must be seen in terms of basic economic institutions. The market in land, by controlling the organic development of communities, not only produces the social, environmental, and esthetic monstrosities we call "metropolitan areas," but removes from the community the creative, synthesizing power that lies at the base of true solidarity. Thus communities become agglomerates of isolated individuals with few common activities and impersonal and apathetic interpersonal relations.

A community cannot thrive when it holds no effective power over the autonomous activities of profit-maximizing capitalists. Rather, a true community is *itself* a creative, initiating, and synthesizing agent, with the power to determine the architectural unity of its living and working spaces and their coordination, the power to allocate community property to social uses such as participatory child-care and community recreation centers, and the power to insure the preservation and development of its natural ecological environment. This is not an idle utopian dream. Many living-working communities do exhibit architectural, esthetic, social, and ecological integrity: the New England town, the Dutch village, the moderate-sized cities of Mali in sub-Saharan Africa, and the desert communities of Djerba in Tunisia. True, these communities are fairly static and untouched by modern technology; but even in a technologically advanced country the potential for decent community is great, given the proper pattern of community decision mechanisms.

The normal operation of the basic economic institutions of capitalism thus render major activity contexts inhospitable to human beings. Our analysis of work and community could easily be extended to include ecological environment and economic equality with similar conclusions.[8]

This analysis undermines Illich's treatment of public service bureaucracies. Illich holds that service agencies (including schools) fail because they are manipulative, and expand because they are psychologically addictive. In fact, they do not fail at all. And they expand because they exist as integral links in the larger institutional allocation of unequal power and income. Illich's simplistic treatment of this area is illustrated in his explanation for the expansion of military operations:

The boomerang effect in war is becoming more obvious: The higher the body count of dead Vietnamese,

[8] See Michael Reich and David Finkelhor, "The Military-Industrial Complex," in *The Capitalist System*, ed. Richard C. Edwards, Michael Reich, and Thomas Weisskopf (Englewood Cliffs, N.J.: Prentice-Hall, 1972).

the more enemies the United States acquires around the world; likewise, the more the United States must spend to create another manipulative institution— cynically dubbed "pacification"—in a futile effort to absorb the side effects of war. [DS, p. 54]

Illich's theory of addiction as motivation proposes that, once begun, one thing naturally leads to another. Actually, however, the purpose of the military is the maintenance of aggregate demand and high levels of employment, as well as aiding the expansion of international sources of resource supply and capital investment. Expansion is not the result of addiction but a primary characteristic of the entire system.[9]

Likewise from a systematic point of view, penal, mental illness, and poverty agencies are meant to contain the dislocations arising from the fragmentation of work and community and the institutionally determined inequality in income and power. Yet Illich argues only:

. . . jail increases both the quality and the quantity of criminals, that, in fact, it often creates them out of mere nonconformists . . . mental hospitals, nursing homes, and orphan asylums do much the same thing. These institutions provide their clients with the destructive self-image of the psychotic, the overaged, or the waif, and provide a rationale for the existence of entire professions, just as jails produce income for wardens. [DS, p. 54]

Further, the cause of expansion of service agencies lies *not* in their addictive nature, but in their

[9] See Gintis, "Power and Alienation," for a concise summary.

failure even to attempt to deal with the institutional sources of social problems. The normal operation of basic economic institutions progressively aggravates these problems, hence requiring increased response on the part of welfare agencies.

The Roots of Consumer Behavior

To understand consumption in capitalist society requires a *production* orientation, in contrast to Illich's emphasis on "institutionalized values" as basic explanatory variables. Individuals consume as they do—and hence acquire values and beliefs concerning consumption—because of the place consumption activity holds among the constellation of available alternatives for social expression. These alternatives directly involve the quality of basic activity contexts surrounding social life—contexts which, as I have argued, develop according to the criteria of capital accumulation through the normal operation of economic institutions.

What at first glance seems to be an irrational preoccupation with income and consumption in capitalist society, is seen within an activity context paradigm to be a logical response on the part of the individual to what Marx isolated as the central tendency of capitalist society: the transformation of all complex social relations into impersonal *quid-pro-quo* relations. One implication of this transformation is the progressive decay of social activity contexts described in the previous section, a process which reduces their overall contribution to individual welfare. Work, community, and environment become sources of pain and displeasure rather than inviting contexts for social relations. The reasonable individual response, then, is (a) to disregard the development of personal capacities which would be humanly satisfying in activity contexts which are not available and, hence, to fail to demand changed activity contexts and (b) to emphasize consumption and to develop those capacities which are most relevant to consumption per se.

Second, the transformation of complex social relations to exchange relations implies that the dwindling stock of healthy activity contexts is parceled out among individuals almost strictly according to income. High-paying jobs are by and large the least alienating; the poor live in the most fragmented communities and are subjected to the most inhuman environments; contact with natural environment is limited to periods of *vacation,* and the length and desirability of this contact is based on the means to pay.

Thus commodity fetishism become a *substitute* for meaningful activity contexts, and a *means of access* to those that exist. The "sales pitch" of Madison Avenue is accepted because, in the given context, it is true. It may not be much, but it's all we've got. The indefensibility of its more extreme forms (e.g., susceptibility to deodorant and luxury automobile advertising) should not divert us from comprehending this essential rationality.

In conclusion, it is clear that the motivational basis of consumer behavior derives from the everyday observation and experience of individuals, and consumer values are not "aberrations" induced by manipulative socialization. Certainly there is no reason to believe that individuals would consume or work much less were manipulative socialization removed. Insofar as such socialization is required to *stabilize* commodity fetishist values, its elimination might lead to the overthrow of capitalist *institutions*—but that of course is quite outside Illich's scheme.

The Limitations of Left-Convival Technologies

Since Illich's views the "psychological impotence" of the individual in his/her "addictedness" to the ministrations of corporate and state bureaucracies as the basic problem of contemporary society, he defines the desirable "left-convivial" institutions by the criterion of "non-addictiveness."

Applied to commodities or welfare services, this criterion is perhaps sufficient. But applied to major contexts of social activities, it is inappropriate. It is not possible for individuals to treat their work, their communities, and their environment in a simply instrumental manner. For better or worse, these social spheres, by regulating the individual's social activity, became a major determinant of his/her psychic development, and in an important sense define *who* he/she is. Indeed, the solution to the classical "problem of order" in society[10] is solved only by the individual's becoming "addicted" to his/her social forms by *participating through them*.[11] In remaking society, individuals do more than expand their freedom of choice—they change *who they are*, their self-definition, in the process. The criticism of alienated social spheres is not simply that they deprive individuals of necessary instruments of activity, but that in so doing they tend to produce in all of us something less than *we intend to be*.

The irony of Illich's analysis is that by erecting "addictiveness vs. instrumentality" as the central welfare criterion, he himself assumes a commodity fetishist mentality. In essence, he posits the individual *outside* of society and using social forms as instruments in his/her preexisting ends. For instance, Illich does not speak of work as "addictive," because in fact individuals treat work first as a "disutility" and second as an instrument toward other ends (consumption). The alienation of work poses no threat to the "sovereignty" of the worker because he is not addicted to it. By definition, then, capitalist work, communities, and environments are "nonaddictive" and left-convivial.

---

[10] Talcott Parsons, *The Structure of Social Action* (New York: Free Press, 1939).

[11] Karl Marx, *The Economic and Philosophical Manuscripts of 1844* (Moscow: Foreign Language Publishing House, 1959), and Karl Marx and Friedrich Engels, *The Germany Ideology* (New York: International Publishers, 1947).

Illich's consideration of the capitalist enterprise as "right-manipulative" only with respect to the consumer is a perfect example of this "reification" of the social world. In contrast, I would argue that work is *necessarily addictive* in the larger sense of determining who a man/woman is as a human being.

The addictive vs. instrumental (or, equivalently, manipulative vs. convivial) criterion is relevant only if we posit an essential "human nature" prior to social experience. Manipulation can then be seen as the perversion of the natural essence of the individual, and the deinstitutionalization of values allows the individual to return to his/her essential self for direction. But the concept of the individual prior to society is nonsense. All individuals are concrete persons, uniquely developed through their particular articulation with social life.

The poverty of Illich's "addictiveness" criterion is dramatized in his treatment of technology. While he correctly recognizes that technology can be developed for purposes of either repression or liberation, his conception requires that the correct unalienated development of technological and institutional forms will follow from a simple aggregation of individual preferences over "left-convivial" alternatives.

The same analysis which I applied to the atomistic aggregation of preferences in the determination of activity contexts applies here as well: there is no reason to believe that ceding control of technological innovation and diffusion to a few, while rendering them subject to market criteria of success and failure, will produce desirable outcomes. Indeed this is *precisely* the mechanism operative in the private capitalist economy, with demonstrably adverse outcomes. According to the criterion of left-conviviality, the historical development of technology in *both* private and public spheres will conform to criteria of profitability and entrepreneurial control. Citizens are reduced to *passive consumers*, picking and choosing among the technological alternatives a technological elite presents to them.

In contrast, it seems clear to me that individuals must exercise direct control over technology in structuring their various social environments, thereby developing and coming to understand their needs through their exercise of power. The control of technical and institutional forms must be vested directly in the group of individuals involved in a social activity, else the alienation of these individuals from one another becomes a *postulate* of the technical and institutional development of this social activity—be it in factory, office, school, or community.

In summary, the facile criterion of left-conviviality must be replaced by the less immediate—but correct—criterion of *unalienated social outcomes*: the institutionally mediated allocation of power must be so ordered that social outcomes conform to the wills and needs of participating individuals, and the quality of participation must be such as to promote the full development of individual capacities for self-understanding and social effectiveness.

Schooling: The Prealienation of Docile Consumers

Everywhere the hidden curriculum of schooling initiates the citizen to the myth that bureaucracies guided by scientific knowledge are efficient and benevolent. . . . And everywhere it develops the habit of self-defeating consumption of services and alienating production, the tolerance for institutional dependence, and the recognition of institutional rankings. [*DS*, p. 74]

Illich sets his analysis of the educational system squarely on its strategic position in reproducing the economic relations of the larger society. While avoiding the inanity of reformers, who see "liberated education" as compatible with current capitalist political and economic institutions, he rejects the rigidity of old-style revolutionaries, who would see even more repressive (though different) education as a tool in forging "socialist consciousness" in the Workers' State.

What less perceptive educators have viewed as irrational, mean, and petty in modern schooling, Illich views as merely reflecting the operation of all manipulative institutions. In the first place, he argues, the educational system takes its place alongside other service bureaucracies, selling a manipulative, prepackaged product, rendering their services addictive, and monopolizing all alternatives to self-initiated education on the part of individuals and small consenting groups.

Yet, argues Illich, schools cannot possibly achieve their goal of promoting learning. For as in every dimension of human experience, learning is the result of personal *activity*, not professional ministration:

Most learning is not the result of instruction. It is rather the result of unhampered participation in a meaningful setting. Most people learn best by being "with it," yet school makes them identify their personal, cognitive growth with elaborate planning and manipulation. [*DS*, p. 39]

Thus, as with all bureaucratic service institutions, schools fail by their very nature. And true to form, the more they fail, the more reliance is placed on them, and the more they expand:

Everywhere in the world school costs have risen faster than enrollments and faster than the GNP, everywhere expenditures on school fall even further behind the expectations of parents, teachers, and pupils. . . . School gives unlimited opportunity for legitimated waste, so long as its destructiveness goes unrecognized and the cost of palliatives goes up. [*DS*, p. 10]

From the fact that schools do not promote learning, however, Illich does not conclude that schools are simply irrational or discardable. Rather, he asserts their central role in creating docile and manipulable consumers for the larger society. For just as these men and women are defined by the quality of their *possessions* rather than of their *activities,* so they must learn to "transfer responsibility from self to institutions. . . ."

Once a man or woman has accepted the need for school, he or she is easy prey for other institutions. Once young people have allowed their imaginations to be formed by curricular instruction, they are conditioned to institutional planning of every sort. "Instruction" smothers the horizon of their imaginations. [*DS,* p. 39]

Equally they learn that anything worthwhile is standardized, certified, and can be purchased.

Even more lamentable, repressive schooling forces commodity fetishism on individuals by thwarting their development of personal capacities for autonomous and initiating social activity:

People who have been schooled down to size let unmeasured experience slip out of their hands. . . . They do not have to be robbed of their creativity. Under instruction, they have unlearned to "do" their thing or "be" themselves, and value only what has been made or could be made. . . . [*DS,* p. 40]

Recent research justifies Illich's emphasis on the "hidden curriculum" of schooling. Mass public education has not evolved into its present bureaucratic, hierarchical, and authoritarian form because of the organizational prerequisites of imparting cognitive skills. Such skills may in fact be more efficiently developed in democratic, nonrepressive atmospheres.[12] Rather, the social relations of edu-

---

[12] The literature on this subject is immense. Illich himself is quite persuasive, but see also Charles E. Silberman, *Crisis in the Classroom* (New York: Random House, 1970), for a more detailed treatment.

cation produce and reinforce those values, attitudes, and affective capacities which allow individuals to move smoothly into an alienated and class-stratified society. That is, schooling reproduces the social relations of the larger society from generation to generation.[13]

Again, however, it does *not* follow that schooling finds its predominant function in reproducing the social relations of *consumption* per se. Rather, it is the social relations of *production* which are relevant to the form and function of modern schooling.

A production orientation to the analysis of schooling—that the "hidden curriculum" in mass education reproduces the social relations of production—is reinforced in several distinct bodies of current educational research. First, economists have shown that education, in its role of providing a properly trained labor force, takes its place alongside capital accumulation and technological

---

[13] Gintis, "Contre-Culture et Militantisme Politique," *Les Temps Modernes* (February 1971), "New Working Class and Revolutionary Youth," *Socialist Revolution* (May 1970), and "Education and the Characteristics of Worker Productivity," *American Economic Review* (May 1971); David Cohen and Marvin Lazerson, "Education and the Corporate Order," *Socialist Revolution* (March 1972); Clarence Karrier, "Testing for Order and Control," *Education Theory* (forthcoming); Michael B. Katz, *The Irony of Early School Reform* (Cambridge, Mass.: Harvard University Press, 1968), and "From Voluntarism to Bureaucracy in American Education," *Sociology of Education*, 1972; Joel Spring, "Education and Progressivism," *History of Education* (Spring 1970); and Robert Dreeben, *On What Is Learned in Schools* (Reading, Mass.: Addison-Wesley, 1968).

change as a major source of economic growth.[14] Level of educational attainment is the major non-ascriptive variable in furthering the economic position of individuals.

Second, research shows that the type of personal development produced through schooling and relevant to the individual's productivity as a worker in a capitalist enterprise is primarily *non-cognitive*. That is, profit-maximizing firms find it remunerative to hire more highly educated workers at higher pay, essentially *irrespective* of differences among individuals in cognitive abilities or attainments.[15] In other words, two individuals (white American males) with identical cognitive achievements (intelligence or intellectual attainment) but differing educational levels will not command, on the average, the same income or occupational status. Rather, the economic success of each will correspond closely to the average for his educational level. All individuals with the same level of educational attainment tend to have the same expected mean economic success (racial and sexual discrimination aside). This is not to say that cogni-

---

[14] See Edward F. Denison, *The Sources of Economic Growth in the United States and the Alternatives Before Us* (New York: Committee for Economic Development, 1962), and Theodore Schultz, *The Economic Value of Education* (New York: Columbia University Press, 1963).

[15] This surprising result is developed in Gintis, "Education and the Characteristics of Worker Productivity," and is based on a wide variety of statistical data. It is validated and extended by Christopher Jencks et al., *Education and Inequality* (New York: Basic Books, 1972).

tive skills are not necessary to job adequacy in a technological society. Rather, these skills either exist in such profusion (through schooling) or are so easily developed on the job that they are not a criterion for hiring. Nor does this mean that there is no correlation between cognitive attainments (e.g., IQ) and occupational status. Such a correlation exists (although it is quite loose),[16] but is almost totally mediated by formal schooling: the educational system discriminates in favor of the more intelligent, although its contribution to worker productivity does not operate primarily *via* cognitive development.[17]

Thus the education-related worker attributes that employers willingly pay for must be predominantly *affective* characteristics—personality traits, attitudes, modes of self-presentation and motivation. How affective traits that are rewarded in schools come to correspond to the needs of alienated production is revealed by direct inspection of the social relations of the classroom. First, students are rewarded in terms of grades for exhibiting the personality characteristics of good workers in bureaucratic work roles—proper subordinancy in relation to authority and the primacy of cognitive as opposed to affective and creative modes of social response—above and beyond any

[16] See, e.g., Jencks et al.
[17] For more extensive treatment, see Jencks et al. and Gintis, "Education and the Characteristics of Worker Productivity."

actual effect they may have on cognitive achievement.[18] Second, the hierarchical structure of schooling itself mirrors the social relations of industrial production: students cede control over their learning activities to teachers in the classroom. Just as workers are alienated from both the *process* and the *product* of their work activities, and must be motivated by the external reward of pay and hierarchical status, so the student learns to operate efficiently through the external reward of grades and promotion, effectively alienated from the process of education (learning) and its product (knowledge). Just as the work process is stratified, and workers on different levels in the hierarchy of authority and status are required to display substantively distinct patterns of values, aspirations, personality traits, and modes of "social presentation" (dress, manner of speech, personal identification, and loyalties to a particular social stratum),[19] so the school system stratifies, tracks, and structures social interaction according to criteria of social class and relative scholastic success.[20] The

[18] For an analysis of relevant data and an extensive bibliography, see Gintis, "Education and the Characteristics of Worker Productivity," and "Alienation and Power" (Ph.D. diss., Harvard University, 1969).

[19] This phenomenon is analyzed in Claus Offe, *Leistungsprinzip und Industrielle Arbeit* (Frankfort: Europaïsche Verlaganstalt, 1970).

[20] See Merle Curti, *The Social Ideas of American Educators* (New York: Scribners, 1935); Gintis, "Contre-Culture et Militantisme Politique"; Gorz, "Capitalist Relations of Production and the Socially Necessary Labor Force," in *All We Are Saying . . .* , ed. Arthur Lothstein (New York: Putnam, 1970), and "Technique, Techniciens, et Lutte de Classes";

most effectively indoctrinated students are the most valuable to the economic enterprise or state bureaucracy, and also the most successfully integrated into a particular stratum within the hierarchical educational process.[21]

Third, a large body of historical research indicates that the system of mass, formal, and compulsory education arose more or less directly out of changes in productive relations associated with the Industrial Revolution, in its role of supplying a properly socialized and stratified labor force.[22]

The critical turning points in the history of American education have coincided with the perceived failure of the school system to fulfill its functional role in reproducing a properly socialized and stratified labor force, in the face of important qualitative or quantitative changes in the social relations of production. In these periods

---

Samuel Bowles, "Unequal Education and the Reproduction of the Social Division of Labor," in *The Capitalist System*, ed. Edwards, Reich, and Weisskopf, and "Contradictions de L'enseignement Superieure" *Les Temps Modernes* (August-September, 1971); and David Bruck, "The Schools of Lowell," honors thesis (unpublished), Harvard University, 1971.

[21] This statement is supported by the statistical results of Richard C. Edwards, Ph.D. diss., Department of Economics, Harvard University, in progress.

[22] Katz, *The Irony of Early School Reform* and "From Voluntarism to Bureaucracy in American Education"; Lawrence Cremin, *The Transformation of the School* (New York: Knopf, 1964); Raymond E. Callahan, *Education and the Cult of Efficiency* (Chicago: University of Chicago Press, 1962); Curti; Bowles, "Unequal Education and the Reproduction of the Social Division of Labor"; Spring; Cohen and Lazerson.

(e.g., the emergence of the common school system) numerous options were open and openly discussed.[23] The conflict of economic interests eventually culminated in the functional reorientation of the educational system to new labor needs of an altered capitalism.

In the mid- to late nineteenth century, this took the form of the economy's need to generate a labor force compatible with the factory system from a predominantly agricultural populace. Later, the crisis in education corresponded to the economy's need to import peasant European labor whose social relations of production and derivative culture were incompatible with industrial wage-labor. The resolution of this crisis was a hierarchical, centralized school system corresponding to the ascendance of corporate production. This resolution was not without its own contradictions. It is at this time that the modern school became the focus of tensions between work and play, between the culture of school and the culture of immigrant children, and between the notion of meritocracy and equality. Thus while Illich can *describe* the characteristics of contemporary education, his consumption orientation prevents him from understanding how the system came to be.

It seems clear that schools instill the values of docility, degrees of subordination corresponding to different levels in the hierarchy of production, and motivation according to external reward. It

[23] See David B. Tyack, *Turning Points in American Educational History* (Boston: Ginn, 1967); and Katz.

seems also true that they do not reward, but instead penalize, creative, self-initiated, cognitively flexible behavior. By inhibiting the full development of individual capacities for meaningful individual activity, schools produce Illich's contended outcomes: the individual as passive receptor replaces the individual as active agent. But the articulation with the larger society is *production* rather than *consumption*.

If the sources of social problems lay in consumer manipulation of which schooling is both an exemplary instance and a crucial preparation for future manipulation, then a political movement for deschooling might be, as Illich says, "at the root of any movement for human liberation." But if schooling is both itself an *activity context* and preparation for the more important activity context of work, then personal consciousness arises not from the elimination of outside manipulation, but from the experience of solidarity and struggles in remolding a mode of social existence. Such consciousness represents not a "return" to the self (essential human nature) but a *restructuring* of the self through new modes of social participation; this prepares the individual for itself.

Of course this evaluation need not be unidirectional from work to education. Indeed, one of the fundamental bases for assessing the value of an alternative structure of control in production is its compatibility with intrinsically desirable individual development through education. Insofar as Illich's left-convivial concept is desirable in any ultimate sense, a reorganization of production should be sought conformable to it. This might involve the development of a vital craft/artistic/technical/service sector in production organized along master-apprentice or group-control lines open to *all* individuals. The development of un-alienated work technologies might then articulate harmoniously with learning-web forms in the sphere of education.

But a reorganization of production has other goals as well. For example, any foreseeable future involves a good deal of socially necessary and on balance personally unrewarding labor. However this work may be reorganized, its accomplishment must be based on individual values, attitudes, personality traits, and patterns of motivation adequate to its execution. If equality in social participation is a "revolutionary ideal," this dictates that all contribute equally toward the staffing of the socially necessary work roles. This is possible only if the hierarchical (as opposed to social) division of labor is abolished in favor of the solidary cooperation and participation of workers in control of production. Illich's anarchistic notion of learning webs does not seem conducive to the development of personal characteristics for this type of social solidarity.[24]

[24] The main elements in Illich's left-convivial "learning web" alternative to manipulative education are all fundamentally dispersive and fragmenting of a learning community:

1. Reference Services to Educational Objects—which facilitate access to things or processes used for formal

The second setting for a politics of education is the *transitional society*—one which bears the technological and cultural heritage of the capitalist class/caste system, but whose social institutions and patterns of social consciousness are geared toward the progresive realization of "ideal forms" (i.e., revolutionary goals). In this setting, the social relations of education will themselves be transitional in nature, mirroring the transformation process of social relations of production.[25] For instance, the elimination of boring, unhealthy, fragmented, uncreative, constraining, and otherwise alienated but socially necessary labor requires an extended process of technological change in a transitional phase. As we have observed, the repressive application of technology toward the

---

learning. Some of these things can be reserved for this purpose, stored in libraries, rental agencies, laboratories, and showrooms like museums and theaters; others can be in daily use in factories, airports, or on farms, but made available to students as apprentices or on off-hours.

2. Skill Exchanges—which permit persons to list their skills, the conditions under which they are willing to serve as models for others who want to learn these skills, and the addresses at which they can be reached.

3. Peer-Matching—a communications network which permits persons to describe the learning activity in which they wish to engage, in the hope of finding a partner for the inquiry.

4. Reference Services to Educators-at-Large—who can be listed in a directory giving the addresses and self-descriptions of professionals, paraprofessionals, and free-lancers, along with conditions of access to their services.

[25] Bowles, "Cuban Education and the Revolutionary Ideology," *Harvard Educational Review*, 41 (November 1971).

formation of occupational roles is not due to the intrinsic nature of physical science nor to the requisites of productive efficiency, but to the political imperative of stable control from the top in an enterprise. Nevertheless the shift to automated, decentralized, and worker-controlled technologies requires the continuous supervision and cooperation of workers themselves. Any form this takes in a transitional society will include a constant struggle among three groups: managers concerned with the development of the enterprise, technicians concerned with the scientific rationality of production, and workers concerned with the impact of innovation and management on job satisfaction.[26] The present educational system does not develop in the individual the capacities for co-operation, struggle, autonomy, and judgment appropriate to this task. But neither does Illich's alternative which avoids the affective aspects of work socialization totally, and takes technology out of the heads of learners.

In a transitional setting, liberating technologies cannot arise in education, any more than in production, spontaneously or by imposition from above. The social relations of unalienated education must evolve from conscious cooperation and struggle among educational administrators (managers), teachers (technicians), and students (work-

---

[26] Marco Maccio, "Parti, Technicien, et Classe Ouvriere dans la Revolution Chinoise," *Les Temps Modernes* (August-September, 1970), and Gorz, "Techniques, Techniciens et Lutte de Classes."

ers), although admittedly in a context of radically redistributed power among the three. The outcome of such a struggle is not only the positive development of education but the fostering of work-capacities in individuals adequate to the task of social transition in work and community life as well.[27]

The inadequacy of Illich's conception of education in transitional societies is striking in his treatment of China and Cuba. It is quite evident that these countries are following new and historically unprecedented directions of social development. But Illich argues the necessity of their failure from the simple fact that they have not deschooled. That they were essentially "deschooled" *before* the revolution (with no appreciable social benefits) does not faze him. While we may welcome and embrace Illich's emphasis on the social relations of education as a crucial variable in their internal development toward new

[27] The theory of political organization which takes *contradictions* among the interests of the various groups participating in the control of a social activity context as central to social development, underlies my argument. This theory is well developed in Chinese Communist thought, as presented in Mao Tse Tung, "On Contradiction" in *Selected Works* (Peking: Foreign Language Press, 1952), and Franz Schurmann, *Ideology and Organization in Communist China* (Berkeley: University of California Press, 1970). In terms of this "dialectical theory of political action," the reorganization of power in education in a transitional society must render the contradictions among administrators, teachers, and students *nonantagonistic,* in the sense that the day-to-day outcomes of their struggles are the positive, healthy development of the educational system, beneficial to all parties concerned.

social forms, his own criterion is without practical application.

The third setting in which the politics of education must be assessed—and the one which would most closely represent the American reality—is that of capitalist society itself. Here the correspondence principle implies that educational reform requires an *internal failure* in the stable reproduction of the economic relations of production. That is, the idea of liberating education does not arise spontaneously, but is made possible by emerging contradictions in the larger society. Nor does its aim succeed or fail according as its ethical value is greater or less. Rather, success of the aim presupposes a correct understanding of its basis in the contradictions in social life, and the political strategies adopted as the basis of this understanding.

The immediate strategies of a movement for educational reform, then, are political: (a) understanding the concrete contradictions in economic life and the way they are reflected in the educational system; (b) fighting to insure that consciousness of these contradictions persists by thwarting attempts of ruling elites to attenuate them by co-optation; and (c) using the persistence of contradictions in society at large to expand the political base and power of a revolutionary movement; that is, a movement for educational reform must understand the social conditions of its emergence and development in the concrete conditions of social life. Unless we achieve such an understanding and use it as the basis of political *action*, a functional reorientation will occur vis-à-vis the present crisis in education, as it did in earlier critical moments in the history of American education.

In the present period, the relevant contradiction involves: (a) blacks moved from rural independent agriculture and seasonal farm wage-labor to the urban-industrial wage-labor system; (b) middle-class youth with values attuned to economic participation as entrepreneurs, elite white-collar and professional and technical labor, faced with the elimination of entrepreneurship, the corporatization of production, and the proletarianization of white-collar work;[28] and (c) women, the major sufferers of ascriptive discrimination in production (including household production) in an era where capitalist relations of production are increasingly legitimized by their sole reliance on achievement (nonascriptive) norms.[29]

This inventory is partial, incomplete, and insufficiently analyzed. But only on a basis of its completion can a successful educational strategy be forged. In the realm of contradictions, the correspondence principle must yet provide the method of analysis and action. We must assess political strategies in education on the basis of the single— but distressingly complex—question: Will they lead to the transitional society?

[28] Bowles, "Contradictions de L'enseignement Superieure," and Gintis, "Contre-Culture et Militantisme Politique" and "New Working Class and Revolutionary Youth."

[29] For a general discussion of these issues, see Edwards, Reich, and Weisskopf, eds., *The Capitalist System.*

I have already argued that deschooling will inevitably lead to a situation of social chaos, but probably not to a serious mass movement toward constructive social change. In this case the correspondence principle simply fails to hold, producing at best a temporary (in case the ruling elites can find an alternative mode of worker socialization) or ultimately fatal (in case they cannot) breakdown in the social fabric. But only if we posit some essential presocial human nature on which individuals draw when normal paths of individual development are abolished, might this lead in itself to liberating alternatives.

But the argument over the sufficiency of deschooling is nearly irrelevant. For schools are so important to the reproduction of capitalist society that they are unlikely to crumble under any but the most massive political onslaughts. "Each of us," says Illich, "is personally responsible for his or her own deschooling, and only we have the power to do it." This is not true. Schooling is legally *obligatory*, and is the *major means of access* to welfare-relevant activity contexts. The political consciousness behind a frontal attack on institutionalized education would necessarily spill over to attacks on other major institutions. "The risks of a revolt against school," says Illich,

. . . are unforeseeable, but they are not as horrible as those of a revolution starting in any other major institution. School is not yet organized for self-protection as effectively as a nation-state, or even a large corporation. Liberation from the grip of schools could be bloodless. [*DS*, p. 49]

This is no more than whistling in the dark.

The only presently viable political strategy in education—and the precise *negation* of Illich's recommendations—is what Rudi Deutchke terms "the long march through the institutions," involving localized struggles for what Andre Gorz calls "nonreformist reforms," i.e., reforms which effectively strengthen the power of teachers vis-à-vis administrators, and of students vis-à-vis teachers.

Still, although schools neither can nor should be eliminated, the social relations of education *can* be altered through genuine struggle. Moreover, the experience of both struggle and control prepares the student for a future of political activity in factory and office.

In other words, the correct immediate political goal is the nurturing of individuals both liberated (i.e., demanding control over their lives and outlets for their creative activities and relationships) *and* politically aware of the true nature of their misalignment with the larger society. There may indeed be a bloodless solution to the problem of revolution, but certainly none more simple than this.

Conclusion

Illich recognizes that the problems of advanced industrial societies are institutional, and that their solutions lie deep in the social core. Therefore, he consciously rejects a partial or affirmative analysis which would accept society's dominant ideological forms and direct its innovative contributions toward marginal changes in assumptions and boundary conditions.

Instead, he employs a methodology of total critique and negation, and his successes, such as they are, stem from that choice. Ultimately, however, his analysis is incomplete.

Dialectical analysis begins with society as is (thesis), entertains its negation (antithesis), and *overcomes* both in a radical reconceptualization (synthesis). Negation is a form of demystification— a drawing away from the immediately given by viewing it as a "negative totality." But negation is not without presuppositions, is not itself a form of liberation. It cannot "wipe clean the slate" of ideological representation of the world or one's objective position in it. The son/daughter who acts on the negation of parental and societal values is not free—he/she is merely the constrained negative image of that which he/she rejects (e.g., the negation of work, consumption order, and rationality is not liberation but negative un-freedom). The negation of male dominance is not women's liberation but the (negative) affirmation of "female masculinity." Women's liberation in dialectical terms can be conceived of as the overcoming (synthesis) of male dominance (thesis) and female masculinity (antithesis) in a new totality which rejects/embodies both. It is this act of overcoming (synthesis, consciousness) which is the critical and liberating aspect of dialectical thought. Action lies not in the act of negation (antithesis, demystification) but in the act of overcoming (synthesis/consciousness).

The strengths of Illich's analysis lie in his consistent and pervasive methodology of negation. The essential elements in the liberal conceptions of the Good Life—consumption and education, the welfare state and corporate manipulation—are demystified and laid bare in the light of critical, negative thought. Illich's failures can be consistently traced to his refusal to pass *beyond* negations —beyond a total rejection of the appearances of life in advanced industrial societies—to a higher synthesis. While Illich should not be criticized for failing to *achieve* such a synthesis, nevertheless he must be taken seriously to task for mystifying the nature of his own contribution and refusing to step—however tentatively—beyond it. Work is alienating—Illich rejects work; consumption is unfulfilling—Illich rejects consumption; institutions are manipulative—Illich places "nonaddictiveness" at the center of his conception of human institutions; production is bureaucratic—Illich glorifies the entrepreneurial and small-scale enterprise; schools are dehumanizing—Illich rejects schools; political life is oppressive and ideologically totalitarian—Illich rejects politics in favor of individual liberation. Only in one sphere does he go beyond negation, and this defines his major contribution. While technology is in fact dehumanizing (thesis), he does *not* reject technology (antithesis). Rather he goes beyond technology *and* its negation towards a schema of liberating technological forms in education.

The cost of his failure to pass beyond negation in the sphere of social relations in general, curiously enough, is an implicit affirmation of the deepest characteristics of the existing order.[30] In rejecting work, Illich affirms that it *necessarily* is alienating—reinforcing a fundamental pessimism on which the acceptance of capitalism is based; in rejecting consumption, he affirms either that it is inherently unfulfilling (the Protestant ethic), or would be fulfilling if unmanipulated; in rejecting manipulative and bureaucratic "delivery systems," he affirms the laissez-faire capitalist model and its core institutions; in rejecting schools, Illich embraces a commodity-fetishist cafeteria-smorgasbord ideal in education; and in rejecting political action, he affirms a utilitarian individualistic conception of humanity. In all cases, Illich's analysis fails to pass beyond the given (in both its positive and negative totalities), and hence affirms it.

The most serious lapse in Illich's analysis is his implicit postulation of a human "essence" in all of us, preceding all social experience—potentially blossoming but repressed by manipulative institutions. Indeed, Illich is logically compelled to accept such a conception by the very nature of his

---

[30] Indeed to stop one's analysis at negation normally leads to implicit affirmation. For a discussion of this, see "The Affirmative Character of Culture," in Herbert Marcuse, *Negations* (Boston: Beacon Press, 1968).

methodology of negation. The given is capitalist (or state socialist) socialization—repressive and dehumanizing. The antithesis is no socialization at all—individuals seeking independently and detached from any mode of social integration their personal paths of development. Such a view of personal growth becomes meaningful in human terms only when anchored in some absolute human standard within the individual and anterior to the social experience that it generates.

In such a conception of individual "essence," critical judgment enters, I have emphasized, precisely at the level of sensing and interpreting one's presocial psyche. This ability requires only demystification (negation); hence a methodology of negation is raised to a sufficient condition of a liberating social science. Dialectical analysis, on the other hand, takes negation (demystification) as the major *precondition* of liberation, but not its sufficient condition. Even the most liberating historical periods (e.g., the Reformation, the French and American Revolutions), despite their florid and passionately idealistic rhetoric, in fact responded to historically specific potentials and to limited but crucial facets of human deprivation. Dialectical analysis would view our present situation as analogous and, rejecting "human essence" as a presocial driving force in social change, would see the central struggles of our era as specific negations *and their overcoming* in localizable areas of human concern—while embracing the ideologies that support these struggles.

The place of critical judgment (reason) in this analysis model lies in a realistic visionary annihilation of both existing society *and* its negation-in-thought in a new, yet historically limited, synthesis. I have argued that this task requires as its point of departure the core economc institutions regulating social life—first in coming to understand their operation and the way in which they produce the outcomes of alienating work, fragmented community, environmental destruction, commodity fetishism, and other estranged cultural forms (thesis), and then in entertaining how we might negate and overcome them through political action and personal consciousness. Illich, in his next book, might leave the security and comfort of negation, and apply his creative vitality to this most demanding of tasks.

All Schooled Up

COLIN GREER

Ivan Illich's new book, *Deschooling Society*, provides a very useful shorthand statement-of-direc-
tion for a society that is "all schooled up," a nice
handle around which to get a grip on the modern
relationship between school and society.

As Illich himself spells it out, "The public is
indoctrinated to believe that skills are valuable
and reliable only if they are the result of formal
schooling." Consequently, the schools have a
monopoly on access to opportunity in society and
the capitalist functions of scarcity and selectivity
are served by the school; meritocracy, the ruling
ethos of modern technological capitalism, is
served by schools in the same way that the doctrine
of divine right was served by the Church. Nowa-
days, the school—the major single vehicle of social selection—replaces other-worldly promises of
the good life with immediate promises of social
mobility and prosperity. At the same time, it helps
to maintain the age-old incongruity between humane democratic rhetoric and monumental social
inequality. Just as with formal religious authority
before it, the school's monopoly on opportunity

goes hand in hand with its oracle status, sustaining the rhetoric of its promises and the conventions of privileged estates by becoming the judge and jury for those wanting "in" on those promises, while rationalizing the exclusion of millions. Jumping from preindustrial to contemporary analogies, Illich likens the public school structure to "the advertising agency which makes you believe that you need the society as it is."

Everyone learns in school how America, from early in the life of the Republic, puts its schools at the heart of its democratic egalitarian promise. The very presence of public schools has become a testament to the glory of the American democratic genius.

Illich takes note of this commitment and its revolutionary origins, but since he makes quite different assumptions about the present, he draws rather different conclusions about the past. The symbol is the same, but the story line is of an entirely different order:

Two centuries ago the United States led the world in a movement to disestablish the monopoly of a single church. Now we need the constitutional disestablishment of the monopoly of the school, and thereby of a system which legally combines prejudice with discrimination. The first article of a bill of rights for a modern, humanist society would correspond to the First Amendment of the U.S. Constitution: "The State shall make no law with respect to the establishment of education." There shall be no ritual obligatory for all.

Illich restates the radical critique and then takes it one step further. Schools monopolize opportunity, he tells us eloquently; they standardize norms and deny individual differences; they delay gratification and kill creativity ("Instruction smothers the horizon of their imagination," he says); they repress love and encourage fear; they teach alienation and competition; and they discourage sharing and cooperation. What Illich calls the "hidden curriculum," the process and content of schooling that successfully ensures that the "products" of the school "have been taught to substitute expectations for hope," diametrically opposes the humane, democratic rhetoric of schools and schoolmen. From elementary school to puniversity, Illich argues, the school apparatus "has the effect of imposing consumer standards at work and at home."

But Illich goes further. Too many critics of public education have failed to understand the subservience of the school monopoly to the social order; rather, they believe, schools have lost their way and can be redirected. "The free school movement," Illich points out, for example, "entices unconventional educators but ultimately does so in support of the conventional ideology of schooling." And so he believes that even many radical figures in the public debate about schools in this country are prisoners of a view of society that equates schooling with education. And to assume the necessity of schools is to assume the necessity of the world that creates them and other major public institutions. In this perspective, "the New World Church is the knowledge industry, both purveyor of opium and the workbench during an increasing number of years of an individual's life. Deschooling is, therefore, at the root of any movement for human liberation."

As Illich explains it, "Equal educational opportunity is, indeed, both a desirable and a feasible goal, but to equate this with obligatory schooling is to confuse salvation with the Church." The critical principle of educational reform is to return "initiative and accountability for learning to the learner or his most immediate tutor."

Unfortunately, when it comes to his vision of the future, Illich is by no means as cogent. He does present the reader with some guidelines for reform practices, but he does not explore the possibility of making those practices represent radical structural changes or take into account the fact that some men are satisfied by the promissory and competitive ethos of the public schools. Of course, for Illich an ideal educational system "should provide all who want to learn with access to available resources at any time in their lives," and technology, he points out, can be a liberating educational method. What he refers to as "skill exchanges," "peer matching," and "reference services"—all designed to make teachers accountable, learners autonomous, and every man a learning resource—should certainly supplement formalized universal access to accredited resources in order to break down exclusionary credentialing patterns and the objectification of persons through teacher/pupil roles.

And yet, reasonable and useful though these guidelines are, the danger of cooptation by the system he opposes, rather than the radical advance he seeks, is as close for Illich as for all the so-called "romantic critics" of schooling. With no theoretical vision of man, no new understanding of man's relationship to the institutions he creates, Illich's reforms can be made to serve the easy commitment to change of more system-oriented reformers. The major purpose of the system is to survive, and reform based on criticisms of current practice usually turns out to be merely a means of survival. Of course, there is a world of difference between Illich and such rationalizers of the system as Charles Silberman, who adopt popular clichés of dissatisfaction in the facile expectation that institutional goals and their outcomes can be changed simply by restating these objectives and what they are intended to achieve. The language of Illich's radical criticism has been easily adapted to the rhetorical platform of those who have constantly diverted our attention from the fact that there is almost no relationship between stated goals and real results.

Illich, aware of this disparity, understands that it is time to look at results in order to get some true notion of what the real—albeit implicit— goals are. But he is not sufficiently aware, at least not in *Deschooling Society*, of the ways in which such critiques as his can serve the system if they ignore the question of why man has created such an institutional structure and what it would really take to change it. There is no historical precedent in the annals of reform to justify hope in the clarion call of criticism and change. Rather, such calls presage future demands by the body politic, and provide the system with guidelines for reforming itself from the inside—so that it can continue business as usual.

The procedures for institutional reform that Illich suggests all add up to a vision of changed institutions, rather than an assessment of how we can—step by step—get from where we are to where he envisions us. The only time he looks at men from the point of view of present world strategy is in his reference to Paulo Freire's educational/political work with Brazilian peasants—at once raising consciousness about their political and economic exploitation and teaching them to read by making political ideology and economic reality the substantive base for literacy training. The only time Illich looks at men from a theoretical frame of reference that is broader than the cogent but limited school/society complex, he identifies it in terms of the tyranny of technological method and the increasing objectification of man since the victory of what he called Prometheus (consumer ethos, planned man-made environments) over Epimetheus (hope, love, and joy). The answer: "While we can specify that the alternative to scholastic funnels is a world made transparent by the communications webs, and while we can specify very concretely how these could function, we can only expect the Epimethean nature of man to reemerge; we neither plan nor produce it."

Illich somehow expects the appropriate transformation simply because he senses—as many of us do—the urging of our moral and cultural breakdowns today. Something has to give, and fast. Now is the time to go one way or the other—humane progress or human holocaust—and Illich has faith in the former. "The mood of 1971 is propitious for a major change of direction in search of a hopeful future."

I am hopeful for the future too, and I believe that we have to make serious choices now. But I am concerned that we won't make the right choices unless we demand greater depth in our social analyses of and recommendations for the institutions we depend on to maintain or remake society.

That schools will change to accommodate new demands is really not in doubt. What is in doubt is whether enough contemporary men will be prepared to respond to new demands in radically new ways. My fear is not that man is dying, but that we will once again miss the opportunity to edit the social script differently. Now, more than ever, we need to examine carefully the relationship of established institutions and the men inside and outside of them to the particular characteristics that make the present unique.

Deschooling in Illich's sense means disestablishing the state, but nowhere is there an analysis of existing theories or the presentation of new formulations of why man has created existing forms of social organization. Without such insight we cannot hope to do more than continue to replicate the bloodiness of revolutionary and counterrevolutionary preening and prancing. Within the wide contours Illich considers essential to an understanding of the role of schools in society, it is dangerous to fall back for solutions on the same kinds of narrow school analyses school people have made for years now; however, instead of reforming them with more money, more personnel, more time, the call here is just as simply and just as narrowly to destroy them—as though somehow schools really were the cause of as well as an effect and an agency of the contemporary social order.

Clearly, Illich is one of the "hopeful brothers and sisters" he would call Epimethean men, who presently represent our best hopes for the future. But human history does not speak highly of the achievement of those marvelous men to date.

Taking Illich Seriously

SUMNER M. ROSEN

Few figures have burst so dramatically onto the American intellectual scene as Ivan Illich. Articles in the *Saturday Review*, the *New York Review of Books*, and the *New York Times* have brought him to the attention of a wide and important audience. *Time* and other mass media publications have bestowed on him celebrity status. From modest beginnings the Intercultural Documentation Center (CIDOC) in Cuernavaca, Mexico, now attracts pilgrims from many parts of the world as both teachers and students. In recent months Illich's campus tours have attracted large audiences and considerable attention. His recent book *Deschooling Society* was widely reviewed. A second book, *Celebration of Awareness*, bringing together various pieces, some written as early as 1956, merited an introduction by Eric Fromm. His article in *Social Policy*, "After Deschooling, What?" (September/October 1971) tries to specify the wider implications of his analysis.

Academics pursuing their steady, undramatic careers tend to be put off by celebrities like Illich, Marshall McLuhan, and Buckminster Fuller. But each man deserves judgment on his own merits. Like the other two, Illich labored for a long time in relative obscurity, confined to journals with limited circulation and appeal. Like McLuhan his more recent fame coincides with a focus on a single central topic and idea. Writing almost exclusively about schools, Illich has simultaneously joined and gone beyond writers like Paul Goodman, John Holt, and Edgar Friedenberg. Unlike them he wants to abolish the schools, not reform them. In this he is alone among major writers on education.

The articles, speeches, and broadsheets that make up *Celebration of Awareness* cover a much wider range of topics and show us a softer, more reflective, and more concretely engaged man than do either the longer and more celebrated *Deschooling Society* or the article grounded in this frame of reference. Illich's observations on the lives of Puerto Ricans in New York, on violence in American cities, on language and silence, and on the Catholic Church in various roles—missionary to Latin America, recruiter and exploiter of priests, social force—are often deep, moving, and eloquent. More than a decade of work of this kind gave Illich credentials that make it difficult not to take him seriously. Celebrity notwithstanding, his position needs to be dealt with rather than dismissed. This is not to say that Illich always hits the target; he does not. But he is on target or close to it enough of the time to merit respect.

The brilliance of his writing, its epigrammatic

and paradoxical weight, poses an obstacle for some. He writes a paragraph where others need pages, a phrase where others need a paragraph. Often the sparks seem to take on a life of their own and to be more distracting than illuminating. He often maps different but converging approaches to his target rather than building a reasoned argument that enables the reader to isolate and deal with the stages of analysis. Illich prefers to state and then restate and elaborate his central insights; he prefers to begin with them rather than to move toward them.

Thus everything depends on the correctness of his position, the accuracy with which his first shot hits the target. In *Deschooling Society* he does not marshal evidence in the usual way, but piles image on image to portray the present system of schooling; with great power he sketches the alternative he would create in its place. It is hard to resist comments like "man must choose whether to be rich in things or in the freedom to use them" (*Deschooling*, p. 62) or his description of how education should work (*ibid.*, p. 75):

A good educational system should have three purposes: it should provide all who want to learn with access to available resources at any time in their lives; empower all who want to share what they know to find those who want to learn it from them; and, finally, furnish all who want to present an issue to the public with the opportunity to make their challenge known.

At the same time one is struck by the heavily theological cast of his writing. Words like "sac-

red," "ritual," "ceremonial," "dogma," and the
like, applied to schools and schoolmen, recur repeatedly. They evoke Illich's theological training
and long work as a priest. They revive and extend
Shaw's early perception of doctors as secular
priests, and they carry weight. At the same time
they run the risk of overstating the case, of carrying both writer and reader too far to be wholly
trusted.

For Illich the school is the world-wide sacred
cow. He dismisses those who focus on the nation-
state or on the corporation as the key instruments
of enslavement or exploitation and as the principal
obstacles to political change. For Illich the political revolutionary simply "wants to improve existing institutions—their productivity and the quality and distribution of their products" (*Celebration,* p. 172). He thinks something far deeper is
needed—institutional or cultural revolution.

The political revolutionary concentrates on schooling
and tooling for the environment that the rich countries, socialist or capitalist, have engineered. The cultural revolutionary risks the future on the educability
of man.

Perhaps some political revolutionaries do want
simply to give the poor what the rich already have,
but this unjust and inaccurate stereotype seems
false to anyone who has listened carefully to the
voices of Black insurgency in the United States.
Writers like Leroi Jones have put the case for rejection of the "sick" white society urgently and
eloquently. Increasingly issues of quality as well as

equality have come to the fore. Illich believes that institutions form not only the character but the consciousness of men and thus the economic and political reality that they are able to imagine and to believe in. He is right to warn the poor and disenfranchised of the world to shun the utopia that universal schooling is advertised as offering and to urge them to put their scarce resources and their hard-won political leverage behind other ways to link work, life, and education. And he is eloquent in sketching what these alternatives can look like; his learning webs, skill exchanges, and reference services (*Deschooling*, ch. 6) are attractive and plausible. Models for them already exist, often unrecognized, and Illich has clearly thought long and hard about how to give them the resources and the credibility that are largely monopolized by the schools he attacks.

But he goes further. For Illich the school, whose "hidden curriculum" is the preservation of privilege and power for the schooled, is the central target in the struggle for liberation.

The hidden curriculum of schools . . . teaches all children that economically valuable knowledge is the result of professional teaching and that social entitlements depend on the rank achieved in a bureaucratic process. The curriculum transforms the explicit curriculum into a commodity and makes its acquisition the severest form of wealth. Knowledge certificates—unlike property rights, corporate stock, or family inheritance—are free from challenge.

If we fail to see that the school is the primary target, he says, we are doomed to fail as revolutionaries, however effectively we deal with the concentration of economic power in large corporations, imperialist domination of poor countries by rich ones, or racist patterns of employment and opportunity (though he does not explicitly denigrate these as targets, they are clearly of subsidiary importance to him). This is not merely an attack on the schools as oppressive and monopolistic; it is put forward as a plan and a path for fundamentally transforming society. And because Illich insists on it, it must be dealt with on these terms.

To him the school is the single source of the fundamental ills that plague all of us. Consider his treatment of Cuba. (*Celebration*, p. 177). He praises Castro's efforts at vastly expanding access to schooling and his concept of the nation as "one big university," which makes formal universities unnecessary.

Yet the Cuban pyramid is still a pyramid . . . there are built-in limits to the elasticity of present institutions, and Cuba is at the point of reaching them. The Cuban revolution will work within these limits. Which means only that Dr. Castro will have masterminded a faster road to a bourgeois meritocracy than those previously taken by capitalists or bolsheviks. . . . As long as communist Cuba continues to promise obligatory high school completion by the end of this decade, it is, in this regard, institutionally no more promising than fascist Brazil, which has made a similar promise. Unless Castro deschools Cuban society, he cannot succeed in his revolutionary effort *no matter what else he does.* Let all revolutionists be warned! [emphasis added]

I do not think I exaggerate Illich's message. What should one make of it? "The hidden curriculum of schools," he argues in *Social Policy*, "has legislated in all the united nations from Afghanistan to Zambia." First, we should note that he intends his analysis to apply everywhere. Highly industrialized, growing, and primitive economies, socialist, capitalist, and mixed regimes, are all called upon to deschool themselves. This boldness is intriguing, but it puts very heavy burdens of proof on the author. Despite great differences, he says, change-makers and revolutionaries in all countries share an infatuation with schooling as the key to their heart's desire—whether it be progress in the case of the poor countries or social justice in the case of the rich ones. Instead, he says, they deliver control over the struggle for these goals to schoolmen, who then have the power not only to control the process but—far more important to Illich—to define the ends to be sought and thus to decide how to reach them. Inevitably the result is that institutions come to control the process, and schoolmen to control the institutions. Therefore, Illich is primarily calling for the dismantling and the removal from power of these institutions; this is his key to liberating mankind.

The pupil is . . . "schooled" to confuse teaching with learning, grade advancement with education, a diploma with competency, and fluency with the ability to say something new. His imagination is "schooled" to accept service in place of value. Medical treatment is mistaken for health care, social work for the improvement of community life, police protection for safety, military poise for national security, the rat race for

productive work. Health, learning, dignity, independence, and creative endeavor are defined as little more
than the performance of the institutions which claim
to serve these ends, and their improvement is made to
depend on allocating more resources to the management of hospitals, schools, and other agencies in question. [*Deschooling*, p. 1]

But the problems confronting the backward
areas of the world are not the same as those facing
major industrial countries. In his almost theological grasp for universals Illich often neglects or
minimizes this fundamental fact. For the developing countries his warnings about education apply
to three major areas of concern: (1) the enormous
costs that are involved in any attempt to provide
universal schooling of the conventional kind; (2)
the key role of schools in perpetuating or recon-
structing a hierarchy of status geared to years of
schooling completed; and (3) the commitment to
existing forms of technology, characteristic of
highly industrialized societies, that is necessarily
implied in the building of a school system; i.e.,
since the only technical education we know is
based on existing methods of production, distribution, and transportation, the only justification for
investing in education is to develop these methods.
The decision to develop along conventional industrial lines is thus implicit in the decision to
create a modern system of education. A fourth
point can be added: those not destined for productive roles in such an economy will emerge
from the schools as consumers; this is a major role
of any system of schooling.

Illich therefore wants to divert the energies now at work in development planning from this set of preoccupations into wholly different directions. He envisages a simple technology and small-scale production, which could combine reasonable levels of productive efficiency with low capital costs, low maintenance costs, and much higher labor-capital ratios than are normally understood as being consistent with "modern" methods of production. His paradigm is a three-legged mechanical donkey— easy to build and repair, cheap to operate, slow but reliable—as the replacement for the tractor in peasant agriculture. Tractors symbolize for Illich all the evils of unquestioned technology. They are expensive to build, operate, and maintain. They are more powerful and more specialized than they need to be. To operate them one must be specially trained, and to maintain and repair them requires still more training; therefore, their use involves expenditures for schools and teachers, thus deepening the peasants' dependence on the school system. Tractors imply large-scale cultivation and thus organized marketing networks, with their concomitant investment in roads, warehouses, and the whole panoply of industrialized agriculture. Illich sees all of this as building new networks of dependence and hierarchy, deepening the subjugation of people to institutions, rather than liberating them from institutional dominance. And he is right to argue that such universal movements are more powerful and decisive than the nominal ideology in the name of which developmental efforts are planned and managed. These are important lessons for those, particularly in Latin America, to whom Illich seems to be most closely attuned and whose problems appear to matter most to him.

Yet it is worth questioning whether the transformation of backward societies through industrialization, even of the conventional kind, does not profoundly alter traditional relations of hierarchy and status, even at the price that Illich attaches to it. Both Japan and the Soviet Union have followed a path that Illich would warn others away from, and the costs have indeed been high in both cases. Yet modernization has been profoundly liberating and equalizing for vast numbers in these countries. Modernization using conventional means does not simply replicate a structure of privilege and status, nor will that be the case in Cuba, to which Illich devotes some attention (he is curiously silent about both the Soviet Union and Japan, though not about Latin America). There is much more to the debate about modernization than the simple model that Illich offers. One must ask whether in Latin America deschooling ranks higher than land reform in the list of tasks to be done.

If we turn to Western industrialized nations, particularly the United States, Illich's case is strongest in relation to those economic sectors furthest removed from direct production—education, health services, social services, criminal justice, mental health, etc. I doubt that he would envisage the dismantling and reconstruction along new, simpler lines of the existing systems of production and distribution in agriculture or industry, though even here there are growing signs that all is far from well and Illich's time may yet come, perhaps sooner than we think. But it is hard to find his scenario credible; however deeply we may wish to modify or reconstuct the political economy of modern industry, this involves far more than Illich is prepared to deal with, at least judging from his available works. There is a pastoral simplicity to Illich's vision of the self-educating, self-sustaining society that Jefferson would have endorsed but that sounds artificial to modern ears. At the same time there is more logic than has so far been acknowledged in the scenario of decentralization and simplification, and increasingly we are being forced to recognize it. Milton Kotler has provided important evidence that the economies of scale may have been vastly exceeded in our patterns of urban government, and John Blair has documented the case for industrial deconcentration and divestiture. Illich does not appear to know their work; his intuitions work well, but he needs to deal more seriously with concrete questions of alternative forms of social and economic organization than he has so far. It is noteworthy that schools have little to do with these issues.

The American industrial empire came to maturity and power without the active collaboration of the sort of school system that Illich makes his primary target. Our present concentrations of

wealth and power protect and extend themselves
in many ways, of which the school may be the
most easily dispensed with. For the survival of
this system schools may have lost the central place
they once had; the workers, technicians, and consumers whose linked lives are the critical keys to
the system can all be formed and captured in other
ways; increasingly they are, which may help to explain why the economic and political powers have
permitted the crisis of learning in our central-city
schools to become so severe without feeling im-
pelled to intervene. Modern industrial production
is increasingly transnational in nature, so that the
failings of the American work force are almost
welcome as excuses to justify the shift of production to Taiwan, Hong Kong, and South Carolina.

Illich is closer to the mark in discussing the
newer, nonindustrial sectors. Here there are already serious problems of cost, quality, accountability, and control of opportunity and privilege;
many of them result from the past control exerted
by the organized professionals whose redoubts are
in the professional schools. Once these professions
were disorganized and inferior, indeed, dangerous
to health and life. Their strength today follows
historically from reforms in the name of quality,
public safety, and reliability, such as Abraham
Flexner's report on medical education, which led
to the reorganization of medical education. Pro-
fessionalization has been a necessary process, but
its elitist character and its domination by organized
groups have seriously, perhaps fatally, flawed the

result we see today that Illich so clearly and correctly chastises.

But can we, in fact, "deschool" the preparation of doctors and lawyers? Clearly we have permitted far too much overschooling; this has been the burden of many recent examinations of medical education, and, indeed, concrete reforms are already under way that will spread with increasing bite in the future. Clearly, too, we have permitted far too much stratification in access to those privileged educational tracks that lead to the medical, legal, and related professions. Equally clearly, institutionalized forms of providing people with "services" are organized far more effectively to serve and perpetuate the interests of these trained providers, and those who train them, than to meet the needs that they ostensibly exist to serve.

But these criticisms do not get at the heart of the matter. The key issue is the degree to which medical education, for example, which Illich would call an institutional problem, can be more accurately seen as a class problem. Doctors are trained in both techniques and in roles, but the roles come first and the techniques derive from them. Doctors could do many things that they do not normally do, though some of them sometimes show that these things are possible. Doctors from the Medical Committee for Human Rights, for example, offered medical services to civil rights workers in Mississippi in 1964, adapting the system of military medicine to serve a social movement. Doctors sometimes join patients in demanding changes in the organization of county or municipal hospitals. They have been known to demand safer automobiles, to work for more effective and widespread preventive medicine programs, to abandon white coats and clinic ambience in order to reach out to groups who need their services but who cannot be reached in traditional ways, and to endorse and participate in mass screening efforts, such as multiphasic screening.

None of these activities corresponds to the roles that form the hidden curriculum of medical education, and all of them require that doctors learn new skills, new roles, and new ways of defining who they are and whom they serve. The methods of diagnosis and treatment that constitute the bulk of their education assume that doctors and patients will normally have certain relatively fixed relations to one another. Eliot Friedson has delineated these in his two recent books;[1] at their core are the roles of the doctor as a dominant figure and of the patient as a passive and presumably grateful recipient. Doctors control the deployment of the array of healing resources, human and technological. They arrange things so that the rich fare better than the poor. They determine research priorities that slight diseases that afflict the poor and the black—sickle-cell anemia —in favor of those that affect the middle classes— heart disease, stroke, and cancer. They reward and

---

[1] Eliot Friedson, *The Profession of Medicine* (Dodd-Mead, 1970); *Professional Dominance* (Atherton, 1970).

thus reinforce standards of behavior that are approved by the affluent and punish those that are disapproved. David Sudnow's study of hospital emergency rooms showed this in one dimension; patients who reek of alcohol or who are shabbily dressed get less serious attention than the well-dressed.[2] Other examples are the uphill struggle to provide funds for an effective attack on venereal diseases and the neglect of the narcotics problem as long as it was confined to black urban ghettos; there are many others.

In short, doctors survive and thrive because they perform class-determined roles in the society. The education that produces doctors and thus admits them to the upper 5 percent of income receivers depends for its support on its continuing ability to reinforce these roles. To ignore class, as Illich does, is to misconceive an important, indeed critical, aspect of the question of whether and how education is linked to revolution. Illich calls for a social revolution, a revolution of institutions, but these institutions are themselves instruments of class purposes, and unless this is made clear his call for revolution cannot succeed.

Strikingly many of the reforms now being discussed and tested respond in their way to Illich's fundamental criticism. Among them are the paraprofessional movement, the community control movement in education, school decentralization and minischools, the replacement of large, imper-

---

[2] David Sudnow, "Dead on Arrival," in *Where Medicine Fails*, ed. Anselm L. Strauss (Transaction Books, 1970).

sonal, remote, and bureaucratic service centers by small, community-based ones, and the development of the therapeutic community to replace the prison or the mental hospital. They involve new ways to recruit, train, and utilize people in the service of other people, challenging the assumptions and the accepted procedures of traditional professional education. They represent efforts to humanize institutions, to widen access to the ranks of those who are deemed qualified to render service, and to shift from peer to client-community scrutiny and accountability. Many of these reforms imply new kinds of education that admit new people, greatly reduce credential tests for status, and—perhaps most critical to Illich's argument—reduce status differences between those who already possess knowledge and those who seek to acquire it and to put it to use. These are serious new efforts. They may not offer the prospect of total transformation of the society, but they are far more than simple reforms accepted in order to preserve existing structures of power and status. As such they need to be taken more seriously than Illich takes them; indeed, they are hardly mentioned in his work.

Should we now accept Illich's advice and abandon the struggle to wrest control of the schools, in the name of a more egalitarian society, from those who have controlled them? Illich seems to be saying that schools cannot be saved, however clever or humane we are; he dismisses as equally ineffective the reformers, the humanizers, and the enthusiasts for local control. Reading these ideas against the backdrop of the struggle since 1954 to end racial dualism in U.S. public education is disturbing. Have all these efforts, some of them bloody and full of tragedy, all of them protracted, dramatic, deeply meaningful to those engaged in the struggle, been in pursuit of goals impossible to achieve because of the very nature of the schooling system itself? Millions of people, black and white, have fought long and hard to create a single system of schooling for all children precisely because they saw the schools as central to the struggle for economic opportunity and social integration. Illich seems to be saying that they were wrong and that even if they won their struggle, would prove in vain. For him schools will always be instruments for socialization into the existing social system, for the perpetuation of a hierarchy based on certified knowledge, for the preservation of monopoly privileges for the schooled minority at at the expense of the less-schooled majority, and for domination of social life by institutions built in the image of the school and controlled by the schooled. A hard and bitter message to ask all of us to accept.

In his argument Illich fails to distinguish issues that must be separated out for analysis. First, he assumes that even if a revolutionary effort wins the struggle to displace those in power and to destroy the institutions of property and privilege that kept them there, the struggle cannot succeed unless the schools are transformed. This in turn assumes that the larger struggle cannot have an important or even decisive effect on the schools, at least to the degree of making their transformation relatively easy. Neither of these assumptions is necessarily valid.

Second, he argues that the struggle to capture the schools and the other social institutions brings closer to realization what I call in the previous paragraph the larger struggle, whether that involves land reform, socialization of industry, expropriation of foreign capital or other "objective" instruments of exploitation. This, too, is not self-evident. Many would argue precisely the opposite case, i.e., that exclusive or primary focus on schools and other social institutions delays and makes more difficult this larger struggle.

Third, he dismisses all reforms of education as simply serving to adapt and thus preserve the existing structure of power and privilege. This argument will appeal to many on the left who see no value in any change short of total revolution. But it totally overlooks the necessity of making day-to-day struggles over proximate objectives a part of the larger, longer, and more difficult process; it ignores the fact that these struggles bring together the potential forces that alone can make basic change possible. These forces do not spring to life of their own accord; they must be built. Saul Alinsky correctly teaches us that this is the secret of all successful organizing efforts; this lesson applies to revolution and to efforts to reach more limited goals.

Yet Illich must be taken seriously, particularly

with regard to the developing economies and to the human services sector of our own economy. His images of educational change—the learning webs; tools, materials, and masters of both accessible to everyone; free choice in what is to be studied, with whom, and when; and acceptance of responsibility for using what one has learned—are extremely valuable as we begin to change our system of education in response to the severe, protracted criticisms to which it has been subjected. These images are profoundly liberating; they will help us avoid replacing one system of domination and manipulation with another.

But deschooling will not solve the major ills of our society, and Illich's claim that it will—that institutional revolution is more central than economic or political revolution—must be rejected. The problem is rather to integrate his agenda with the traditional one, which, focusing on the *forms* of economic and political power, has neglected the question of *process* through which men, once liberated, can realize what they have gained, can protect it, can decentralize power so that no future effort to recapture it can succeed, and can take the responsibility for their own human development fully on their own shoulders. For guidance in these tasks all of us who are serious about social change must be grateful to Illich and must endeavor to engage him further in discussion that will lead toward linking these separate agendas for change.

After Illich, What?

JUDSON JEROME

I have probably learned as much from Ivan Illich as from any author I have read in the last five years. Again and again his brilliant analyses have set me back on my heels and made me look at the world anew. Unfortunately he is better at analysis than synthesis. In particular, his analysis of the dangers of deschooling is as persuasive as his analysis of the dangers of schooling. After reading his article, "After Deschooling, What?" I felt, as I often do after reading his work, furiously paralyzed. I was not furious at Illich, but at the social situation he so lucidly describes. I felt that not only were we unlikely to attain the society he envisages—of self-motivated learners fulfilling themselves with free access to tools, persons, and assemblies—but I was even without strong desire to get there.

Even if the dangers of premature deschooling could be avoided, nothing he suggests addresses the overwhelming social problem he defines:

School is the initiation ritual to a society oriented toward the progressive consumption of increasingly less tangible and more expensive services, a society that relies on worldwide standards, large-scale and long-term planning, constant obsolescence through the built-in ethos of never-ending improvements: the constant translation of new needs into specific demands for the consumption of new satisfactions. This society is proving itself unworkable.

Laissez-faire education runs the same risks as laissez-faire economics. Power and privilege accumulate like an avalanche. There must be safeguards, regulations, guarantees of opportunities, and these themselves perpetuate the system. Compulsory education was invented to help equalize opportunity, to even the score, to prevent exploitation. To some extent it has done so, but at the same time it has created deadening standardization, artificiality, and, as Illich often points out, a new system of hierarchy and privilege as oppressive as the one it was meant to displace.

If we simply closed down the schools, oppression would increase, as the prosperous and ambitious would accumulate more and more power and those less fortunate or those numbed by their social background would be trodden under. You can guarantee access, but little more (as we learn daily from our system of compulsory education). Nor is the problem merely credentialism. Illich writes:

The discrediting of school-produced, complex, curricular packages would be an empty victory if there were no simultaneous disavowal of the very idea that knowledge is more valuable because it comes in certified packages and is acquired from some mythological knowledge-stock controlled by professional guardians.

True enough. But even if there were, magically

(e.g., by religious conversion), such a widespread "disavowal," there is no reason to believe that social equality would result.

I have known for many years that if I wanted riches and power I might learn something about investment, banking, real estate, or business. Nothing prevented my learning such things. There are books in public libraries and magazines; I could get low-rung jobs that would lead to greater knowledge. But I have never had the slightest inclination to pursue these opportunities because acquisition of such wealth and power is simply not a high priority in my vision of the good life. Similarly, the poor in this country may have limited opportunities to participate in the system and may be oppressed even further to the degree that they are compelled to serve time in the schools; but even if these inequalities and injustices were ameliorated, they would not likely be motivated to "take advantage" of their "opportunities." The system sucks. "This society is proving itself unworkable," as Illich says. To join it eagerly is a kind of madness.

Illich also very clearly recognizes that changing the educational system is only a part of a much larger political and economic agenda. He talks about "the joy of conscious living" as a goal.

The learner must be guaranteed his freedom without guaranteeing to society what learning he will acquire and hold as his own. Each man must be guaranteed privacy in learning, with the hope that he will assume the obligation of helping others to grow into uniqueness.

But that hope is vain and the guarantees are worthless unless there is some social structure that supports and rewards such values. Behind deschooling I see emerging a whole range of alternative institutions, regulations, stipulations, guarantees, and other vain props that bring us no nearer joy nor conscious living. Even a guaranteed annual wage (which I generally favor) is an empty gesture in a society that contains little worth buying, in a civilization ravaging the planet like cancer and providing little innate satisfaction even to the fattest cancer cells.

Education is a positive force—a function that cannot be performed merely by providing freedom and sensitive advisement or by ensuring access to tools, resources, and people. It occurs willy-nilly, by chance or planning—at the mother's breast, in the locker room, in the ghetto streets, in kitchen drudgery, and in school servitude. As Illich sees so clearly, much of the "content" of what is learned comes from the context, the environment, the emotional climate, rather than from any stated curricular. In simpleminded but well-meaning efforts to provide good education through schooling we have largely ignored precisely those surrounding factors that teach more than teachers and books. And the major factor—again as Illich recognizes —is compulsion. Compulsory education, like compulsory love, is a contradiction in terms. Where there is compulsion a person can learn, but he learns mostly about compulsion rather than reading, writing, and arithmetic. He learns to be docile or rebellious; he learns to sit still for long hours without thinking; he learns to fear or hate or be sickeningly dependent upon authority figures. Surely that element of education must go. If schools remain (be they "free" schools or traditional ones) the first business of the day should be to establish clearly and unequivocally that anyone is free to leave—the classroom, the school—whenever he wishes, and that there are real alternatives, places to go, things to do, that are safe, stimulating, authorized.

However, like Illich, I see schools as educationally counterproductive, no matter how much they are reformed, radicalized, or liberalized. In trying to figure out how to cure the ills of colleges and universities I moved first in the direction of creating utopian alternative institutions—imagining society peppered with group dynamics people—facilitators, as they are called—resource banks, agents, institutes, retreats, and what have you, replacing colleges and schools altogether. This sounds very much like the social design Illich proposes.

But I have more recently realized that you cannot get there from here. It is not a deschooling but a deinstitutionalizing of society that is called for. The history of Western civilization can be written in terms of the gradual encroachment of institutions on familial, community, and individual life. We have become passive filaments acted upon by specialists—from barbers to psychoanalysts to surgeons to lawyers to mechanics—alienated not only from our labor, but from our bodily functions, our food and drink, our transportation, our children and spouses, and our elderly, living as Peter Seeger described us, in boxes, in lives made of ticky-tacky. This will not change merely through our demanding and getting freedoms, equality, guarantees, resources. The system thrives on that process, eternally producing more legislation and more cadres of professionals to administer more and more funds, programs, plans—and institutions.

The social revolution that is already underway does, indeed, call for a deschooling of society, but it demands the replacement of schools with new learning contexts—humane, loving, supportive, and fully integrated with ongoing life. Old and young together, gardening, sewing, baking, repairing cars, and rediscovering one another, life processes, their relation to the earth and fellow people. Publicity for a recent conference on communes announced:

The family has changed greatly with the industrial revolution, slowly losing its basic functions to other institutions—the functions as the fundamental unit for work, for education, for the care of the elderly and infirm, and now to a large degree for child rearing and for emotional support. More than 40 percent of a large city's population is no longer attached to families, and much of the rest is only very loosely so. Our basic social unit is sorely strained and often fractured. If we can't go home, can we build a new one, better adapted to our new and changing conditions?

Intentional families and communities are one means of providing a context for education without schools. Another goal of the social revolution is to break the consumerism cycle, to find greater satisfaction in the processes of living and loving than in buying goods and services. Liberation from an addiction to consume will free a good deal of energy for fuller engagement with family and community, for working the earth, wiring a house (or learning to enjoy alternatives to electricity). In Illich's writing, education is often strongly linked to vocation, but I can imagine our moving toward a society in which very few people have vocations other than being people. The whole propelling myth of progress, advancement, achievement of material success, already disenchants large numbers in our society—and the disenchantment is spreading. Instead of holding jobs to earn the money to buy hi-fis and records, people may take leisurely hours to sing and make music together. Similarly most of our perceived "needs" are the products of conditioning by the system. And to a large extent we can educate ourselves to recognize and respond to other needs—deeper, more natural, more spiritual, less expensive and destructive, more integrated and humane.

This is a subtle but vast educational task. Obviously it is not one for texts or teachers or programs or data banks. Very little education, I believe, has to do with the acquisition of skills or objective knowledge. It is more the shaping of attitudes, beliefs, values, patterns of satisfaction, creativity, more the releasing of springs of energy and mind. I believe we are only beginning to see how—after the era of schooling—we can address ourselves to education in this larger sense. I have no faith that simply let alone, to use what resources he will, man will educate himself to be nonacquisitive, nonaggressive; that he will stumble on an integrated life; that he will be stimulated to profound searching and inquiry and creativity, to caring and enduring relationships with others, to a wise use of the earth, to a concern for survival of his species and the investment of energy and commitment to that end. I know that one cannot impose these values—by school or church or other prescriptive means. I do not believe it is a job for professional educators—except in the sense that we are all, perpetually, educators of ourselves and one another. But I see it as a conscious, deliberate task, not to be relinquished irresponsibly.

The Case for Schooling America

ARTHUR PEARL

Ivan Illich refuses to define his "desirable society" or to defend its feasibility. Instead of setting forth a set of goals and the logic for same, and a strategy that at least offers a promissory note for payoff, he parades before us metaphor and hyperbole that are—when analyzed—either contradictory or trivial. Any dream of a good life offered by a responsible critic should have at least: (1) its attributes sufficiently spelled out so that advocates and opponents know what they are arguing about; (2) its essence analyzed for ecological, political, psychological, and economic reality (which, of course, could then be debated); and (3) its political course laid out so that we are alerted to the tactics and strategy needed to get us from where we are to where we ought to be.

Illich doesn't come close. He is fuzzy about his "desirable society." He touches on freedom of the individual to learn whatever he desires to learn; he touches on the question of universal and unlimited access to the secrets and tools of the society. But he never discusses the feasibility of his good society. He believes that by the elimination of

compulsory education, the good society will somehow emerge.

Illich never tells us how his improved society
will function without institutions. Indeed, he in no
way challenges my own belief that no steps toward
what he and I might well agree are the goals of
a "desirable society" can be taken without institutions. Public schools will be basic to this institutional infrastructure directed toward widescale social benefits. Illich's call for deinstitutionalized
schools in a deinstitutionalized society is nonsense,
and dangerous to the extent that its simplicity is
attractive.

Deinstitutionalize a city and within a month that city
will literally be buried in its garbage. To have a deinstitutionalized natural society in which man main-
tained himself through self-sufficient primitive hunting,
fishing or gathering would require that we reduce the
world's population to something less than 200 million
people.

It remains true, however, that although schools
do not run society, they are more resistant to society's attempt to run them than are most other
institutions. The fact is that our schools are not
monolithic; people do not emerge from them as
sausages out of a meatpacking plant.

True educational reform inside and outside
schools is really possible, then, because the schools
themselves do not have an already established or
predetermined monopolistic role. They offer a
variety of experiences and interests and provide a
place for increasing numbers of "radical" teachers

to function. It is, after all, only among persons with many years of compulsory education that Ivan Illich has any following—and that is not an accidental occurrence. Schools develop intellectual opponents to injustice not because they are designed to, but because once a group of inquiring youths are compelled to interact with each other, a percentage will begin to question the values and direction of their society. Thus it was the students and teachers in public institutions who first questioned the war in Vietnam; and efforts to restrict them, though powerful, cannot succeed.

Oh, for a Schooled Society!

It will not be easy to create schools with a democratically oriented leadership that convinces rather than coerces people to acknowledge the importance of education. And yet that challenge cannot be avoided either by the dehumanizing experts of education (B. F. Skinner and the like) or the humanely oriented romanticists (Illich and his buddies). Universal education is necessary and must be organized because the threats to man's existence are universal. What we have come to regard as human rights can be guaranteed only within an institutional structure—societies with primitive institutions never even considered individual rights.

The rights of students must be considered

within a context of social responsibility. If the student chooses to be in a classroom rather than a library, laboratory, park, museum, home, or pool hall, he must justify that or the other choices within the context of the goals of a desirable society. He must make a case, with logic and evidence, that he has fulfilled his obligations to other human beings; he has equal rights to require that teachers and colleagues justify their actions to him.

But when Illich speaks with the voice of pure freedom, he masks a conservative message: ". . . protect the autonomy of the learner—his private initiative to decide what he will learn and his inalienable right to learn what he likes rather than what is useful to somebody else." To learn what one likes is to learn prejudices. If there is one thing we know about human beings it is that they don't want to know what they don't want to know. Erich Fromm tried to get that truth across to us twenty years ago in *Escape from Freedom*. The important truths of today are painful truths. People will do everything they can to avoid them. Important truths will require enormous changes in attitudes and life-style. Education self-selected will be no education—we have such education currently available to us (it comes to us on half a dozen simultaneous channels on television), and there we find a Gresham's law of culture: bad drives out good, and the frivolous outdraws the serious.

The institutional school has not, of course, been

relevant to producing a "desirable world"; that is why it must be reformed. Schools must go beyond merely raising the problems; instead they must begin to suggest real solutions—describe models and plans for peace, a universal quality of life, and equal opportunity, within the context of life styles that are ecologically sane. Rather than eradicate the public school, then, Illich ought to be directing his fire against the powerful institutions—the ones C. Wright Mills identified as military, industrial, and political—that block the progressive potential of the schooling process.

The public schools are clearly in desperate shape. Reform won't come easily, and we have a long way to go. Illich and other critics provide a useful function when they hammer away at the schools' inhumanity; but they become counterproductive when they offer nonsolutions and lose sight of the Gideon's army of radical public-school leaders whose growing number has greatly contributed to the clamor to do something about war, racism, poverty, and the destruction of earth during the past decade. Try to deinstitutionalize education as a symbol and the beginning of the deinstitutionalization of everything and you *reinstitute the law of the jungle*—which quickly breaks down into a new set of oppressive institutions. The same unfortunate situation holds true for attaining any of the other goals of a desirable society. Politics learned at the hands of Richard Daley, culture picked up at the feet of Johnny Carson, and interpersonal relations gleaned from gropings in the street are the alternatives to school. That these alternatives are already too characteristic of contemporary American society is not a reason for removing schools, but for reforming them.

Need for a Risk Quotient

ROY P. FAIRFIELD

It is difficult to take issue with Ivan Illich's analysis of the need for deschooling society. Nor can I disagree that people of every age should be free to determine what they should learn and the ends toward which such knowledge might lead . . . without contracting social mortgages. Too, one applauds Illich for counseling caution, lest we deschool society so rapidly that the proverbial cure be worse than the disease. But we need to take a closer look at the assumptions about people implicit in both the analysis and the recommendations. Further, we need to take a hard look at several kinds of risk deschooling implies.

As a humanist I certainly *believe*—in the tradition of Rousseau, nineteenth-century libertarians, and contemporary Third Force psychologists—that men become free as they *act* freely. Individuals are legion who demonstrate such self-verification. But the record is murky regarding groups that have freed themselves. Although some groups, usually with a hard faith or program, have found ways to release themselves from the host culture or subculture, they have often done it in the context of hostility, alienation, and even annihilation.

There is certainly little optimism to be gained from the historical record; and there is no record of a mass society such as ours turning itself around in as radical a way as deschooling demands. And although the accomplishment of such an "impossibility" may be the only goal worth seeking, probability speaks against it. For it seems safe to predict that establishmentarian keepers of the keys are more likely to throw the keys overboard than to unlock the gate. It may be true that things must get sicker before they get any "weller"; but has enough thought been given to the matter of social and psychological risk, in both macrocosmic and microcosmic terms? How rapid a rate of change can we manage? Who, if anybody, will do the managing? Or will the change come willy-nilly? Who will be humanized by the processes? Dehumanized? How much will result from thoughtful, experimental policy formation? Can we avoid changes by default? Or, in the tradition of the clash of political and social forces, will change result from factions in action? Those concerned with the problem will have little difficulty asking a thousand more such questions.

Macrocosmic Perspectives

The social consequences of too quick a deschooling are obvious. Few families have either the fiscal or physical resources, to say nothing of the psychological resources, for sponsoring a year-round school holiday. Nor, granting parents' social conditioning over the past several decades, is it possible to conceive of wide and creative use of imagination sufficiently rapid to preclude a more horrible fate for children than is now evident. And though our complex and relatively resilient federalism always has managed to muddle through most local, state, and national crises, it is obviously incapable of coping with incipient anarchy. In fact, it is reasonably safe to predict that repression might come so swiftly as to make the Dark Ages look like an arctic summer!

It is also highly unlikely that *any* legislative body in the United States is going to reverse its general tendency toward nonaction in tax reform, tortoise-like propensity for avoiding hard issues, and general disinclination to assume a radical posture. Further, think of the face that would be lost, even if money were saved (yet to be proved), if legislatures had to admit that they might have been wrong all these decades in supporting the public schools . . . however chintzily!

Unless we metamorphose our national character overnight, we are more than likely to back into deschooling, willy-nilly . . . or even via the routes Illich recommends. In a society such as ours, in which, it appears to me, *both* the economy and the technology are out of control (assuming they were ever in!), such a process as deschooling would be relatively unpredictable both as to rate of change and management—despite the rising tide (fad?) of accountability! In the spirit of faction-formation and its history in this country (see James Madison's tenth *Federalist* paper, written in 1787), deschooling would probably result from first one group, then ten, and still ten more forming, testing their limits of imagination and freedom, then perhaps collapsing or being coopted by those in power in a complex, industrialized, urbanized, technologized, and politicized society. This is not to debunk such a process: in fact, would it not be extraordinarily ironic and/or paradoxical if huge corporations as well as big government were to organize deschooling!

No; it is doubtful if deschooling would be either swift or sweeping.

Some Microcosmic Risks and Concerns

Risks to individuals, to families, and to other small groups may be as grave as those to the larger society. And here I speak on the heels of seven years of working closely with students up to their elbows in experimental and experiential learning.

Few have dealt enough with the risk factors of this kind of education, risks positive, risks negative, and risks in between. Naturally, those deeply engaged are true believers and assume that the results will be positive; and there is a large body of evidence to prove their point: self-verification, growth, fulfillment, self-actualization, all blossom splendidly in the lush climate of freedom. Free schools, inner colleges, field trips, work-study programs, encounter configurations—all are perceived as humanizing in their impact; and, considered existentially, it doesn't really matter too much whether any of these programs have much longevity. A commune, for instance, should not be measured (as utopian communities have been measured in the past) by its capacity to endure. Indeed, one human insight in such a context may be "worth" a thousand teachers' salaries! And to those critics of Dr. Spock's "permissiveness" or the failure of John Dewey, one might respond that such a conclusion is as nonsensical as determining the worth of a sunset. The germ of fulfillment grows from the belief that taking such risks is worthwhile.

It is relatively easy to recite specific cases to illustrate belief-for-me, but one may be sufficient: A black woman, an elementary-school teacher, held the hope of breaking into college teaching, a wish to know her people better, the desire to meet some of the great black scholars of our time, a fantasy about going to Africa. But it all seemed so hopeless that she wasn't sure she even wanted to talk about it on that May day. When she approached me about the possibility of pursuing a graduate degree, incorporating some of these hopes and wishes in her program, I simply said, "Why not!" Today, she is on the near side of *all* those experiences.

But there are ample cases of those on the far side, of students unable to bridge the chasm between their own rhetoric about free-form learning

and their ability to accomplish such ends. So conditioned are they to being told what to do in
school, so geared to routinized approaches to learning, and so used to perceiving learning as a particular kind of experience to be had in specific
locations and within narrow parameters that their
very confrontation of self in attempting to evolve
a *self*-directed strategy becomes in itself a threat.
And the threat often leads to paralysis, and paralysis to something worse, perhaps *anything* worse!
One such threat, which I saw at fairly close range,
seemed to land a student in a mental hospital.
Another led to reversion to alcoholism. And another and another and. . . . Suffering from their
own disbelief, students often return to some style
in which they are more comfortable, stew in their
own guilt, project their impotency onto persons
perceived as authority figures ("You are forcing me
to be free!"), or perhaps drop out.

Predictability Matters

And there is an unpredictability here that almost
defies application of the most sophisticated anxiety
and/or ego-strength scales. Who can predict surely
on the basis of past *school* performance whether or
not an urban teacher or community-action intern
will be able to face his own whiteness or his own
blackness if he is caught in racial crossfire? Who
can predict, given both subtle and not-so-subtle
cultural conditioning, whether or not a person

over fourteen can manage the cross-cultural and/ or cross-subcultural tensions in settings such as the Peace Corps, Action, or Vista programs, in which, theoretically, a learning quotient should be very high? The record of the volunteers in both the Peace Corps and Vista, even when millions of dollars have been spent to "develop" flexible people, is hardly a paradigm for a deschooled society! The dropout rate from the Peace Corps has steadily climbed; hence the promises of a new, exciting, and potentially *opening* experience are no guarantee that a person will make the most of it.

Those convinced that the American family is dying will not argue too strenuously with the observation that married adults entering experiential learning matrices (encounter groups of all types, universities without walls, communes, external-degree programs, etc.) may run a greater risk of separating from spouses than those in more rigid and traditional programs. After all, the youth culture offers ample illustration of such eventualities. Furthermore, why get uptight about it if it is the wave of the future? And there is more group support for that person who wishes to use such learning matrices to justify the ending of a bad engagement or a bad marriage. Doesn't the group support only manifest the person's "rightness"? Result: conflict whose dimensions are unpredictable.

But assuming that taking risks, with unpredictable outcomes, is perceived as being "good" for the person, regardless of social consequences,

how does the so-called educator, facilitator, teacher
—call him what you will—*encourage* risk? Does
he have any responsibility in encouraging risk in
the face of sure or probable catastrophe even when
the learner insists that he wants to be free to work
out his own destiny? Does he have such responsibility when paranoid or schizophrenic behavior is
evident or likely to be induced by the very climate
of tension or threat in which the learner and
facilitator are involved? Too, what dimensions of
risk-creativity-risk catastrophe does the facilitator-
by-what-ever-name (on the parkway, in a factory,
at a work bench, wherever) face in a deschooled
society that he did not face when he stood, sat, or
even lay before a class of thirty or three hundred?
Will facilitators in the deschooled society become
more like the entrepreneurs of the golden age of
American capitalism—daring, bold, imaginative,
expedient? May they not also risk self-aggrandize-
ment? And if they do, will that humanize or de-
humanize those whom they are encouraging? Is it
not possible that they will end up reinventing
school? Because if they seek to control, they may
discover it necessary to handle persons in increasingly larger groups, and how can they do that without reproducing the kind of society they want to
maintain? And is it likely that were this to happen,
they would become aware of a basic paradox, that
the closer one is to the center of power, the less he
has to achieve his ends?

Then, of course, there are other paradoxes the
deschoolers must face: Will learning cost less if

social expenses decline while individual costs rise? What risk is there if a person sees group support as a prerequisite to gaining strength so daring will increase? What are the tactics and strategies for programming oneself to be free, to verify self? How can the advocates of deschooling guarantee that the managers of such a process will master the art and science of appreciating irony, paradox, and humor and—this being their major task—put themselves out of business?

New Coordinates

Not only have schools in this country taught students to tell time and measure lines, cubes, and spheres but such activity tends to symbolize the four dimensions of a commonsensical society. A deschooled society will need to expand those dimensions so that its citizens will search for coordinates in space-time-psyche-intuition and perhaps ten more dimensions. Programs that are firm, identifiable, and predictable will give way to processes more describable by calculus than geometry. It will become increasingly anachronistic to identify learning with places such as P.S. 107, Harvard, Iowa State, or the Sorbonne. Ironically, those really struggling to learn may become more risk oriented than security minded since learning really *is* dangerous—if one acts upon his learning. It will become increasingly nonsensical to search for groups that may last a lifetime: that is already an anachronism, despite the energies of thousands of alumni secretaries, *treasurers*, and other womb-seeking graduates. Rather, groups in a deschooled society will be greater in number, shorter in duration, and more intense in activity. Also, ironically, they could become more human if threats of longevity, recrimination, and absorption disappear and uniqueness is appreciated by all those who participate in any learning situation.

In short, we'll need new definitions of and attitudes toward the *where* coordinate of learning. We'll need appreciation of the alternative meanings of *time* if an individual learner is encouraged to evolve his own time rhythms outside the context of sixty- or fifty-minute hours. When the walls are really pushed out of the schools and the overhead, administrative, and teaching superstructures and chimneys collapse, we'll be freed from the post-lintel system that has boxed us in for so many centuries. Possibly we can create organic structures in which to keep warm (ironically: womblike) or keep snow and rain off our heads . . . if we can somehow manage the coordinate of *place* in the context of relative time in the larger gestalt of psyche-intuition pushing us into far-out ways of learning ways of conceiving, ways of perceiving. Too, although the traditional disciplines of mathematics, chemistry, history, and literature, to name only a few, may serve as *referents*, they must be perceived, used, and manipulated as just that—*referent*—not as absolutes in any sense whatever. Otherwise, evolving new and freer forms of seeing the who, where, when, and why will be an exercise in futility.

And if we deschool: In the beginning there will be risk; in the process there will be risk; and no man will miss the risk of rebirth in the dying. But if he gets that far, he may find excitement and satisfaction in the daring to dare.

And It Still Is News

MAXINE GREENE

"After Deschooling, What?" may not be Ivan Illich's most eloquent or most logically structured piece of writing, but it is in many ways exemplary. In addition, it is a kind of portmanteau, carrying assorted notions previously displayed. We are familiar by now with the "hidden curriculum," the attack on credentialism, the stress on "precooked knowledge," the connection between privilege and specialized tools. But this article does something else as well, and this is what preoccupied me. Presenting not the slightest evidence that he has read the literature of education, Illich picks out the very problems with which educational researchers and philosophers have been concerned for at least fifty years and displays them, as if for the first time, before our (presumably horrified) eyes. He is obviously entitled to do this for his own purposes, but I find it difficult to understand how people who *are* familiar with the literature can react to Illich's reports upon the schools as if he were bringing the news that God is dead.

Take, for instance, the concept of knowledge as commodity. There is no evading the grim fact that many teachers *do* still purvey what Whitehead called "inert ideas"; nor is there any point in denying that many still impose their subject matter as if it were some "official reality" to be unquestioningly absorbed.

Anyone who has even sampled the literature, however, is aware that this problem has been of primary concern in American education since William James's *Talks to Teachers* and John Dewey's earliest pedagogical works. Knowing as directed inquiry, as participation, as cognitive action: the point has been repeatedly made year after year. Piagetian research, Bruner's inquiries, the analysis of mind and language by logical empiricists, the existential concern for knowing as *praxis:* on all sides people have been stressing what Illich offers as a radical proposal. "I believe," he writes, "that only actual participation constitutes socially valuable learning. . . ." Indeed, yes. But why do teachers stand up and cheer when they hear it from his lips?

A somewhat different point can be made about his conviction that children are entitled to a free choice of *what* and *how* they learn. Few would disagree about the importance of the learner's "free determination . . . of his own reason for living and learning." If we want to motivate, if our teaching is aimed at helping children learn how to learn, we naturally try to create situations in which they will reach out on their own initiative—in fact, begin to teach themselves. But what teacher can seriously accept the idea that each individual has an "inalienable right to learn what he likes"? Whence derives such an inalienable right? And why is the only alternative learning "what is useful to somebody else"?

John Dewey, discussing the difference between the enjoyed and the enjoyable, the desired and the desirable, wrote (in "The Construction of Good"):

The fact that something is desired only raises the *question* of its desirability; it does not settle it. Only a child in the degree of his immaturity thinks to settle the question of desirability by reiterated proclamation: "I want it, I want it, I want it."

Teachers are aware, at least on some level, that young people require the kind of guidance that will enable them to perceive the consequences of what they "like," to view it in its interconnections, to make a value choice. Suppose a child does not "like" multiplication; suppose he "wants" to learn how to play the drums and nothing more. He has a *right*, as many have said, to prefer pushpin to poetry; but he is certainly entitled to understand what pushpin signifies and the degree to which it will equip him to cope with a complex world.

Wherever education proceeds, a tension results from two acknowledged needs: to guide and to set free. The pendulum swing has been repeatedly described: the schools move back and forth between prescriptiveness and permissiveness; one or the other is always being tried. Is there a teacher anywhere, outside the radically "free" schools, who does not realize that the job of educating *in part* involves initiating—into the prevailing way of life, some discipline or another, sensitivity to the arts? Even in the British "open classroom," as we are now being reminded by Joseph Featherstone and others, there is a deliberate effort to move children toward more and more disciplined inquiry. Featherstone makes the point that "interests are not just there, like flowers waiting to bud: they are formed and cultivated by good teaching." And what experienced teacher has not come to this conclusion after a few weeks in an urban classroom, or in the sophisticated ambience of some suburban school?

Yet, perhaps because of the dark overtones of "initiation ritual," perhaps because of his emphasis on consumerism, packaging, and the rest, Illich entrances teachers by insisting on what they do not (in real life) believe. But, then, who would dare *not* despise the bourgeois who whispers "Plastics!" to that young man in *The Graduate*? Teachers, particularly the emancipated ones who crowd in to hear Ivan Illich lecture, are as eager to be "with it" as anyone else. "Commodity," "consumption," "privilege," "programming," "manipulation": these are all code words by now, at least for those who claim to possess "Consciousness III." They are words calculated by now to evoke a conditioned response.

Pop Educationese

I have no interest in whitewashing the schools or in defending the system—surely not a system that deliberately plots (and then lies about) the destruction of Vietnam; conducts massacres (and then lies about them) in such places as Attica; pollutes, represses, and demeans. I do tend to believe that the schools compose what Marcus Raskin calls a "channeling colony," intended (by many who control them) to break people down into personnel, to provide them with the kind of specialized knowledge needed for the support of a pyramidal authority. I believe—as both Illich and Raskin suggest—that too many of us are defined by a relationship like that of the colonizer-colonized. Nevertheless, I remain astonished at the willingness of teachers (who know better) to accept what Illich says as the solution.

They are cognizant of the fact that there has been a tragic discrepancy between the dream of equality and personal freedom and the reality. They know, if they have read any educational history at all, that the school has customarily functioned as a selecting-out agency and as a support for the status quo. They realize that there are many sorts of "hidden curriculum" and that the one Illich highlights (the one that "demands that people of a certain age assemble in groups of about thirty under the authority of a professional teacher, etc.") may be the least damaging of all. Most of them have read Paul Goodman and are familiar with the origins of the attack on the "compulsory"; they have read Edgar Z. Friedenberg, and know well the meaning of "processing" and "lower-middle-class values." And if they have not read Jacques Ellul or Herbert Marcuse, they still know (if mainly from Charles Reich) about the depredations of "technique," the manipulations by the media, the menace of the "false consciousness" that makes a man *think* he needs what is worst for him. None of what Illich is saying, therefore, comes as a surprise.

The only thing that *has* come as a surprise is the term that must have been intended to *épater la bourgeoisie*—the term "deschooling." And, oddly enough, it has been seized upon primarily by those who make their living in or around the schools. It is my impression, in fact, that great numbers of the general public (trade unionists, taxpayers, school board members, community board participants, neighborhood councils, business associations) have never heard of Ivan Illich. When I mention deschooling to nonacademic friends, I must admit, they stare blankly; and when I explain, they shrug.

My hypothesis is that Illich (who thinks of himself, with some justice, as a gadfly) has been providing occasions for "consciousness-raising" for assorted educators. After lectures at the Center for Intercultural Documentation (CIDOC), people are much inclined to speak plaintively of themselves as "schooled." They are mainly teachers saying *mea culpa* before preparing to begin the new term at school. There appears to be something cathartic, something purgative about the experience of castigating the schools when the schools are conceived as "independent variables," *the* determinate institutions in the consumerist society. Also, there is something titillating to a teacher's ego in becoming aware that he, whose professionalism has been so often questioned, is a reluctant Atlas holding the System on his shoulders. (There is something more than titillating about the consequent thought that if he shrugs or sneezes or laughs aloud, the System may slide off his fragile shoulders and crack to pieces on the ground.)

Mea Culpa or Radical Change?

There may be (and I hope this is the case) an increase in self-consciousness and in critical awareness after an exposure to Illich. His purpose may truly be to goad people into wide-awakeness, to make them see. Whatever the variety of schools, I believe the teacher who is sincerely "radical" has the capacity to move his students to do their own kind of critical learning—at higher and higher levels of complexity. I think he has an obligation to teach them the use of the cognitive tools they need, to acquaint them with the principles that structure the disciplines, and to offer the disciplines (which are modes of ordering experience, modes of sense-making) to each one as live possibility. I think he also has an obligation to present himself to his students as a questioning, fallible, searching human being (his fellow human beings); to break through the secrecy of certain specialties (the "inaccessibility" Illich so rightly criticizes) by engaging his students and himself in the most rigorous, open-ended thinking they—and he—can do.

Of course, it helps to attack old "idols." It helps to expose the cracks in the system; it even (sometimes) helps to mock the Establishment, to tweak its tail. But I think we have to keep our eyes on the outraged and the disinherited as well as on the "small, cowardly, and hedonistic"; I think we have to listen, as we have never listened before, to the demands for human dignity (and decent food, housing, jobs, even classrooms). I think we have to *learn* more about transforming institutions and improving environments.

I do not think that oppressiveness, and consumerism, and racism, and violence can be overcome through changes in personal consciousness divorced from institutional stances. I do not think it will be enough to reconceive our reality and our "democratic personality," to *see* differently, as so many young "dropouts" apparently see. It will be necessary to come to terms with power conceived as something other than "personal growth" —the power of the state, which at some point must be expected to change hands. I do not believe deschooling will ensure that happening; I do not believe that "dialectic encounter," no matter how rich, can compensate for the alienation experienced in the corporate society *or* lead to the taking of power in any significant sense.

My Ivan Illich Problem

NEIL POSTMAN

To you, Ivan Illich (*Social Policy*, September/October 1971) may be the most exciting social critic since Marshall McLuhan swept down from the North Country; but for someone like me—an education reformer with a past and a few plans for the future—Ivan Illich is a big headache.

For openers, he has forced me to acknowledge how much more conservative I am than I had thought. Since Illich swept up from the South Country, I have been obliged to admit to unsuspected attachments to certain social structures, which attachments a genuine revolutionary like Illich has obviously abandoned. As a matter of fact, several times in recent months I have returned soberly and respectfully to a passage in the Declaration of Independence that I had previously been inclined to dismiss as merely a conservative cliché:

Prudence, indeed, will dictate that governments long established should not be changed for light and transient causes; and accordingly all experience hath shewn, that mankind are more disposed to suffer while evils are sufferable, than to right themselves by abolishing the forms to which they are accustomed.

Substitute the word "schools" for "governments," and the passage is entirely relevant to the matter at hand. A world without schools? Without students? Without teachers? Without Jewish holidays? Without summer vacation? Without diplomas? Well, it is one thing to criticize—even hate —the school establishment. But it is quite another not to have one at all. And I am not so sure, as I once was, that I like the possibility. For someone like me, who has been characterized as a "radical" and a "dissident," the discovery of such a wide streak of institutional dependence is quite surprising and, of course, troublesome.

But not nearly so troublesome as another problem Illich raises for me—the question of intellectual cowardice or, even worse, obtuseness. After all, it is perfectly plain that Illich's ideas about deschooling society are merely the logical extension of almost all the important criticisms made of the schools during the past five or six years. One could not have read, say, Paul Goodman or Edgar Friedenberg or Jules Henry without sensing, at some level of one's understanding, where it was all pointing. Here, for example, is a passage from my own book, *Teaching as a Subversive Activity*, in which there is a listing of some of the ideas the "hidden curriculum" teaches:

Passive acceptance is a more desirable response to ideas than active criticism.
Discovering knowledge is beyond the power of students and is, in any case, none of their business.
Recall is the highest form of intellectual achieve-

ment, and the collection of unrelated "facts" is the goal of education.

The voice of authority is to be trusted and valued more than independent judgment.

One's own ideas and those of one's classmates are inconsequential.

Feelings are irrelevant in education.

There is always a single, unambiguous Right Answer to a question.

English is not History and History is not Science and Science is not Art and Art is not Music, and Art and Music are minor subjects and English, History and Science major subjects, and a subject is something you "take" and, when you have taken it, you have "had" it, and if you have "had" it, you are immune and need not take it again. (The Vaccination Theory of Education?)

Now, here is a passage from Illich on the hidden curriculum:

The traditional hidden curriculum of school demands that people of a certain age assemble in groups of about thirty under the authority of a professional teacher for from five hundred to a thousand times a year. It does not matter if the teacher is authoritarian so long as it is the teacher's authority that counts; it does not matter if all meetings occur in the same place so long as they are somehow understood as attendance. The hidden curriculum of school requires—whether by law or by fact—that a citizen accumulate a minimum quantum of school years in order to obtain his civil rights. . . .

The hidden curriculum teaches all children that economically valuable knowledge is the result of professional teaching and that social entitlements depend on the rank achieved in a bureaucratic process. The hidden curriculum transforms the explicit curriculum into a commodity and makes its acquisition the securest form of wealth.

The two obviously go together. And even if Illich's goes deeper, it is surely implicit in my own passage that the problem is not simply that schools are bad, but that schooling is bad. Why, then, didn't I say that? Did I pull back for some reason? Why did I shun the consequences of an assault on the institution itself? Well, one does not like to think of oneself as cowardly or stupid, so naturally I can offer several rationalizations. One is that John Holt, Jonathan Kozol, George Dennison, and all the others who produced the pre-Illich literature of education discontent pulled back, too. Or at least didn't explicitly say what I am assuming must have been in everyone's mind—that deschooling is the answer. But a better rationalization is that it wasn't in everyone's mind at all, including my own, that it took a social critic of Illich's brilliance and peculiar cultural detachment to move criticism of education to another and deeper level.

In any case, you can see what a problem Illich is. He not only makes one feel conservative and obtuse: he also makes one wonder about the value of past efforts and future plans. Am I part of the problem? Does my work obscure the real issues? Every time I actually help a school to improve on its treatment of children, do I also help to perpetuate the hidden curriculum?

These are nasty questions to ask oneself, but naturally I have tried to answer them. It hasn't been easy, but it has been most satisfying, especially because, for the moment, I have been able to lay Illich to rest. If Illich has been a problem for you, too (but especially if he hasn't—that is, if you are inclined to think he has the answer), then you may be interested to know just how I am presently coping with my Ivan Illich problem.

Mysticism and Utopianism

To begin with, in spite of his considerable capacity for rigorous social criticism, Illich is essentially a mystic—which is not in the least objectionable so long as his congregation acknowledges the realm in which he dwells. In this case, as with other mystics, like B.F. Skinner, his realm is the purely hypothetical. For example, in proposing a deschooled society, Illich offers an alternative that, like the City of God, is invulnerable to criticism. It is invulnerable because it does not exist and, in the form he proposes, has never existed. Thus, once we have gone beyond the boundaries of faith, how can we say that a deschooled society is either good or bad, or even somewhere in between? How do we know if it is better or worse than what we have?

We cannot say, and we do not know. Now, in most experimental or innovative situations, especially where there are no precedents, we must give the same answer. But it is very important to say that there is a vast, qualitative difference between what Illich has in mind and some education experiment such as a university without walls or a school within a school. Most innovations are attemps to correct a specific evil. One tries them, criticizes them, and then determines how much good they do. If they do not work, one tries something else, and then something else again if that doesn't work. Experimentation also occurs within a reasonably stable framework, which presumably remains intact if an experiment fails.

But Illich is not talking about experimentation or innovation. In fact, he is explicit in saying that such efforts represent a superficial approach. He is a *totalist*, not an experimentalist. He is offering a new order, a complete package, which requires the restructuring not merely of education but of all other social and political institutions. Moreover, the absence of any real (as opposed to hypothetical) perspectives from which to criticize his proposal—even from which *he* can criticize his proposal—does not in the least disturb Illich. In other words, like most mystics, he is also a utopian. That is why he does not warn us about things that might go wrong. Or discuss the psychological impediments to the success of his system. He assumes, with Skinner, that if we change the environment —in this case, totally—we will get exactly the kind of "human nature" we have planned for.

Perhaps. But it is deeply to be doubted. On paper, all utopian schemes look good. Even our present schooling process does not fare badly—on paper. No one would guess from the way schools are usually described in catalogs or curriculum guides how elitist they are, or how destructive to intelligence, or how authoritarian. Yet they are, and it is not out of place to ask how they got that way. Is it that teachers and administrators are evil? Did they design their certificates to ensure mediocrity? Did they all conspire to gang up on the poor? Well, in theory they didn't. It worked out that way because people are imperfect; and once their imperfections become systematized, it is very difficult to remedy them.

But where are the imperfections in the world Illich envisions for us? Will there be no elitism, no meanness, no bureaucracies, no hierarchies, no inequities? If he expects them, Illich says nothing, perhaps because he is thoroughly entranced with the power of his plan to deliver us from evil.

What about the Poor?

Of course, I am leading up to saying that Illich is not only a mystic and a utopian but an authoritarian as well. In spite of his deep concern for the process of education, he has almost nothing usable to say about the process of change generally, or about the process of achieving a deschooled society in particular. What he calls political objectives— no compulsory attendance, no discrimination on the basis of prior attendance, and the transfer of tax funds from institutions to people—taken together with his three radical demands amount to a definition of a deschooled society. Beyond this, he proposes no strategies, rules of discourse, questions, restraints, modes of conduct, or anything else that would help to achieve a change of such magnitude. This is not surprising, for Illich's eye is firmly fixed on the goal, which fixation is the essence of authoritarianism.

Like Skinner (again), Illich is really not interested in process. For instance, he takes no cognizance whatsoever of how the process of getting where he wants us to go will affect where we end up. And he shows no great interest in consulting with the people who would be most affected by such a scheme.

Consider, for example, his attitude toward the poor. Illich is certain that the present schooling process conspires against the poor and the disenfranchised. He virtually assures us (and them) that in a deschooled society such inequities as presently exist will disappear. But this is not how the poor see it—at least, not those I have spoken with. Ask them if they want to do away with schools; if they want, instead, a network of peers, and skill models, and educational resources; if the institution of school has lost all its legitimacy. They will tell you that what they want is better schools and better teachers, and control over both—to which Illich, I suppose, must reply that the trouble with the poor is that they just don't know what's best for them. Perhaps not. Reality doth make clods of us all, which makes it awfully tough for utopians.

This brings me to the most serious complaint that can be lodged against Illich, which is that, *insofar as he means to be taken literally,* his proposal is irrelevant. It is roughly analogous to one's saying that the Vietnam war would end tomorrow if only we Americans would take the message of Christ seriously. That is undoubtedly true. But it ain't gonna happen, so we'll have to find another way. Assuming Illich is correct in his analysis, so what? American society is not going to be de-schooled! Not in the near future, anyway—and for the very reason Illich sees so clearly: the schools function to perpetuate the established order. If Illich thinks that *Griggs* v. *Duke Power Co.* will turn this around, he needs some reality therapy.

There are about 45 million children presently attending public schools in America. At least the same number will still be there ten years from now. If, in any sense, their education will be better than what we have, it will be because the public schools have been improved. Piece by piece. Agony by agony. Not very exciting or revolutionary, to be sure; but that's the way it will happen, if it happens at all. And if Illich disagrees with that, he should at least be advised that most Blacks, Puerto Ricans, Chicanos—the dispossessed generally—don't.

Moreover, it is right on this point that Illich, whether he would approve or not, will be most useful in the years ahead. The clods, the piecemeal reformers, the people without a grand vision, those who are simply trying to improve the quality of the experience that real children have in school, will coopt Illich. (And why not?) He will be heeded, but as one heeds an inventive poet, not a political revolutionary (as Illich would probably prefer). Whether he likes it or not, he will be our Tolstoy, not our Lenin.

In the late summer issue (1971) of *Outside the Net*, Illich's associate Everett Reimer has, in fact, outlined exactly how this might be done. After describing what he calls the Illich-Reimer Alternative, he suggests (almost as if acknowledging its fantasy content) that their proposal can also be used as a basis for evaluating practical innovations and experiments until such time as the world is ready to get serious. The Illich-Reimer proposals, in other words, can be transformed into a series of questions whose answers can be used as a measure of whether or not some specific innovation is moving in the right direction: Will the innovation make resources more widely available? Will it tend to deemphasize the importance of teaching as against learning? Will it tend to make students freer, and their learning less confined?

Thought of as a standard of judgment rather than a serious political proposal, the deschooled society becomes a metaphor, an image, an ideal that provides a basis for intelligent criticism of practical reform. For example, recently New York City's Chancellor Harvey Scribner announced a plan by which high school dropouts could receive "credit" for work experience and thus qualify for diplomas. An interesting idea. How do we judge its intentions? Well, Illich would probably disapprove of the part of the idea that implicitly accepts the legitimacy of diplomas. But much of the rest he would accept since it represents a change toward valuing individual choice, toward using wider resources, toward making an institution responsive to people, rather than the other way around.

How do we evaluate the use of paraprofessionals, or the growth of free schools, or the use of students as teachers, or the reduction of record-keeping, or the elimination of grades, or a university without walls, or, for that matter, homogeneous grouping, contract teaching, behavioral objectives, etc. The imagery and logic of Ivan Illich have something important to tell us about each of these things, provided we understand the level of abstraction at which they are useful. If, on the other hand, we take Illich at a literal level, he may in the end do more to obstruct change than to advance it. For in the face of what he is saying, what true believer can in good conscience do anything about the schools except try to destroy them?

So it comes down to this: Tomorrow, there are going to be about 45 million kids showing up for school. Schooling as an institution may or may not be dead, which is a question that makes for swell lectures in Cuernavaca. But the kids certainly aren't dead. They are *there*. And what happens to them tomorrow matters—and next term, and the term after that. And it just won't do to write them off. Not by me. Because as I see it, some part of some of their lives is my problem. And if Ivan Illich isn't interested, then I figure that's *his* problem.

After Deschooling, Free Learning

RONALD GROSS

"My grandmother wanted me to have an education, so she kept me out of school." Margaret Mead's lovely quip lights up the Illichian mindscape like a flashbulb. Illich has driven a conceptual wedge between the two ideas we have mistakenly fused together under the rubric "Education"—the idea of schooling, and the idea of learning.

When the log splits under the Ockham's ax of Illich's analysis, the two pieces fall apart.

One of the pieces is the institution of schooling; the other is the individual as learner. The space between them is revealed as dry rot. "I see human perfection in the progressive elimination of the institutional intermediary between man and the truth he wants to learn." Berkeley, Columbia, and Paris witnessed the dry rot bursting into flame. What the students were seeking was that direct relationship to truth, that authentic mode of being and knowing, that Illich aspires to.

We know a good deal about the institution of schooling (though not much of what we know is useful in changing things for the better). But the literature of education is virtually devoid of studies of individual learning in its real-life context. Go to the local education library and see what's there. You will find books on school administration, on curriculum, on teaching methods, on the sociology and economics of education. Try to find a book on individual learning, on education outside schools, on how to learn by yourself.

Illich's basic concern in "After Deschooling, What?" is the means by which the individual might reclaim command of his own education: its conception, planning, conduct, evaluation, and use. Having looked back at the historical myth of schooling, and then having looked around at the pernicious effects of present-day "established" education, Illich now looks forward. He is propelled now by "a much deeper concern" than in his previous critical analyses. His concern is "the manner in which learning is to be viewed." The issue is the creation of new "institutional arrangements that protect the autonomy of the learner, his private initiative to decide what he will learn and his inalienable right to learn what he likes rather than what is useful to somebody else."

For the past year, I have been watching closely and to some degree participating in the development of programs that endeavor to do this and examining new ideas and policy recommendations that advocate the approach. The concept of "free learning" sums up for me the cumulative thrust of these developments and their promise for the future. "In its final and positive stage [deschooling] is the struggle for the right to educational freedom." Thus Illich presaged, in his "Constitution for Cultural Revolution," the phase he now enters. For me, educational freedom means free learning.

Schools are not going to shrivel up and blow away; and it is unlikely that they will be "disestablished," as Illich demands. There are too many good ones—and more now than ever before, with the alternative free school system available for those who can't stomach public education.

Rather than a showdown between the "deschoolers" and those who still seek radical reform of schools, I sense that we are involved today in a various, halting, impulsive, sometimes violent groping toward better ways of learning, growing, developing our potentials. My hope is that through the gradual weakening of the constraints of schooling we will so loosen its fabric, and so strengthen the opportunities to learn from other sources, that it will become impossible to separate learning from life, and student and teacher from friends learning together. For this we need a real flowering of other options, other avenues to growing up, other milieus in which to become more human.

Schools themselves would benefit from the creation of numerous options to the present monolithic system, because it would relieve them of the two most disheartening conditions of their work: trying to teach students who don't want to learn in the school's way, and attempting somehow to squeeze a complete education into the limited time and space of schooling. But the primary beneficiaries would be the children. It is for their sake that we are called upon to disenthrall ourselves from the myth of schooling and to cultivate diverse alternatives for lifelong learning and broad-based growth.

These alternatives—increasingly available both in educational theory and in nascent practice—reveal that learning is more individual than we have thought, more varied in its expression and occasion, more evenly spaced along a person's life. An hour's reflection will reveal that each of us learned the most useful, loveliest things he knows outside school. Life, libraries, and labor are potent teachers that leave school and college far behind. The most important learning can, is, and should be personal, voluntary, and concomitant with living. This is *free* learning—unconstrained by time, space, privilege, or legal coercion.

What distinguishes free learning? Why is it important to establish its preeminence as a criterion for other educational experiences? Free learning is that natural human activity which so struck Aristotle: man's unremitting urge to see, know, experience, understand, and master his world.

It is evident in the child, whose sole motivation for learning is often the inherent delight of the process. It is therefore not surprising that one of the most promising applications of Illich's ideas may be in preschool education. Remarkable pragmatic confirmation of this possibility has just been offered by Earl Schaefer, former Chief of Early Child Care Research at the National Institute of Mental Health. In the late 1960s Schaefer directed an infant education project in Washington, D.C. in which infants in poor families were tutored at home an hour a day, five days a week. Mental scores registered a significant gain between fifteen months and three years of age.

But Schaefer now considers this work misguided, because of the even better results obtained by Phyllis Levenstein in New York City through an even freer methodology. Instead of sending paraprofessionals into the home to bring service to the child, the Levenstein project gave parents about a dozen books and a dozen toys and demonstrated how they could be used to promote verbal interaction between a parent and a child. With 32 visits over a 7-month period, she registered a 17-point I.Q. gain. That was equivalent to the effects of the Schaefer project over a 21-month period with over 300 visits.

Based on these empirical findings, Schaefer has come to the conviction that an Illichian approach, focusing on resuscitating the power of the family to provide for its own educational needs, is vastly preferable to the present strategy of extending school programs downward to reach younger children.

Among people of all ages free learning, as a psychological phenomenon, is much more prevalent than we tend to think. A pioneering study by Allen Tough, in Canada, discovered that among 66 adults 65 had conducted at least one self-initiated "learning project" in the past year, with an average of 8 distinct projects totalling 700 hours a year of involvement. Fewer than 1 percent of these projects were motivated by academic credit, and about 70 percent were planned by the learner himself. Ten 16-year-olds and ten 10-year-olds were also interviewed, and a parallel discovery of significant nonschool learning activity was made.

We have literally schooled ourselves out of our capacity even to recognize the prevalence and validity of noninstitutionalized learning. The assertion that free learning is the modal form of education implies that it is *schooling*—with its inordinate set of constraints and limitations—that is the deviant form of education.

It is my conviction now that the norm in learning is not represented by the image of the youngster, in a special institution, learning from teachers, but rather by the adult fully participating in the world, learning from the process of living the fullest possible life.

Consider the multitude of constricting conditions that characterize virtually all schools, everywhere, contrasted to the characteristics of free learning. Schools are legally compulsory, not voluntary; age bound, not lifelong; subject centered, not person centered; book oriented, not experience oriented; teacher centered, not learner centered; competitive, not collaborative; bureaucratically fixated on grades, credits, and diplomas, not mastery oriented; controlling of behavior, not responsive to needs; invidious and advantageous, not equalizing and compassionate.

Free learning does take place today in some schools. But certain inherent characteristics of schools (such as those indicated above) make free learning difficult or impossible. Moreover, the dominance of schools (in terms both of funding and of social imagination) invalidates the vast amount of free learning that takes place *outside* schools and thereby inhibits the full flowering of nonschool, free learning opportunities.

It is not necessary to abolish schools in order to have free learning. But it is necessary to place schools in their proper perspective, to judge them against the standard of free learning (not vice versa, which is now the case), to reform them radically to meet this standard, and to assure the equitable support of nonschool opportunities when they can conduce to free learning better than increased support of school programs.

Impulses in this direction now seem pervasive in American education. The Carnegie Commission on Higher Education has urged that we break the lockstep from high school to college, making it possible to get off the escalator but to get back on later, after a few years of working. The ideas of Goodman and Holt about breaking the monopoly of the schools and strengthening other ways of growing up are being taken seriously. The viability of self-education—a potent American tradition stretching from Benjamin Franklin and Lincoln, through Emerson and Carnegie, down to Eric Hoffer and George Jackson in our time—is being reaffirmed. The voucher system and other schemes for placing educational resources in the hands of consumers—learners—rather than institutions are gaining force. The assumption that virtually all the money available for education should be funneled through the educational establishment is under attack in Congress and in the U. S. Office of Education. The meritocracy of diplomas and credentials is being challenged by young professionals in law, medicine, teaching, and other fields. The equation of school certificates with employability has been dealt a mortal theoretical blow by Ivar Berg's study *The Great Training Robbery* and by the Supreme Court's recent decision in *Griggs v. Duke Power Co.*

These theoretical and policy findings are being translated into practice by such initiatives as the Parkway "school without walls" in Philadelphia, Sesame Street, the "growth centers" on the East and West Coasts, Britain's new televised Open University, the *Whole Earth Catalogue*, the new "learning communes," the "university without walls," New York State's nonresidential adult college for independent study, and the free school movement. The message of all of these is clear: there are beautiful options, finer possibilities, more natural, economical, just, humane, and potent means of education available to us than schooling as we have known it.

As the editors of *Manas,* the journal of humanistic psychology, point out in a recent examination of Illich's ideas, deschooling does not mean the elimination of meeting places between teachers and learners. It means facilitating in all practicable ways the sharing of information and skills. It should conduce to a vast burgeoning of contact points, comparable to the expansion from the present system of broadcast television to the cable system, which would permit a thousand programs to feed into each receiver at a given moment.

This last point well illustrates how the Illichian perspective forces us to look at our "educational" problems in broader terms. For it is precisely through technological breakthroughs like cable television that free learning can be made possible. "Once we take as problematic the issue of who does the teaching and where it takes place, new possibilities open up for us." Most of those possibilities lie in the area we now label "communications" rather than in education.

It will become increasingly obvious over the next five years, I believe, that educational policies and communications policies are inextricable, and that in the most important instances the former should be subsumed under the latter. "The alternative to scholastic funnels," Illich says in *Deschooling Society,* "is a world made transparent by the communications webs."

Indeed, if learning is to be lifelong and "lifewide," voluntary and various, then changes in all our other institutions will be necessary. Once we

acknowledge (as has every great educational the-
orist from Plato to John Dewey) that it is the
culture, the *paideia,* that truly educates, then we
will swiftly conclude that present American culture mostly miseducates.

The most potent teachers of our day are not in
the schoolrooms. They are the masters of the mass
media, the major professions, government, those
who design our cities, organize our work, make
our music and movies. The great educational experiences of the last ten years for Americans—children and adults—have been the civil rights, anti-
war, and women's movements. The great educational issue this year is not the financial plight of
schools and colleges, but the clandestine carving-up
of the empire of cable television, the last great
hope for reclaiming the video wasteland.

We are caught, then, on the horns of the Pla-
tonic dilemma. If only the whole society educates,
and our society at present either fails to educate
or miseducates, how shall we lift ourselves by our
own bootstraps? The answer lies in the capacity
of individuals to surpass their culture, to conceive
finer possibilities of learning and growth, and
then to teach the rest of us by their example. Society is a wonderful mechanism for preserving and
transmitting what is already known; but it cannot
grow, it cannot produce something new. For that,
we must look to individuals.

That is where Illich looks. By turning, in "After
Deschooling, What?", to learning and the learner,

he is calling for a revolution in our arrangements for education that is epochal in scope. It is comparable with the shift from tribalism and an oral culture to a written one that stored and transmitted knowledge through books. It is as bold, theoretically, as the second great revolution in Western education, which strove to put the student rather than the teacher at the center of the process of education. Now, Illich calls for a third revolution: liberating the learner from the institutionalized context altogether. The way to an educative society, he maintains, is not through ever-more-powerful institutions, but through a revival of the potency of learners.

That is why Illich finds the heart of the matter in how we must change the basic concept of learning and of knowledge and their relationship to the freedom of the individual in society. "It is in the name of education that we must get rid of the school." He could well add that it is in the name of the individual that we must reaffirm our control over our own learning, repossess the capability to shape our minds, revive the potency of our intellectual and creative faculties.

Because our thinking about learning has been dominated for so long by the image of the school, we know virtually nothing about the potentialities for truly individual learning, or about how the other institutions of a society can become adjuncts to and resources for the learning process. We do not know why some people continue to learn and grow while others do not. We do not know, except in the still-rare cases of autodidacts, the potentialities for truly individual learning.

Even worse than these lacunae in knowledge is the atrophy of our collective imagination. We can only dimly envisage how the major institutions of society could become accessible resources for learning. We do not know, in short, how to seize back for the individual the power over the growth of his own mind, or what to do with that power once we gain it.

But we do know that the problem of education today cannot be solved by schools and colleges. There is too much to know and understand—not just from books, but from conditions, from life, from love and struggle. Like birth and death, the true act of learning is ultimately individual. But without the conditions provided by other people and by humane institutions, it will not occur.

Illich affirmed his commitment to this view at a seminar in December 1970 at the Ontario Institute for Studies in Education. Seemingly seized by a conviction that he had achieved his apogee in articulating his views on education, Illich told the chairman of the meeting that this was the last time he would speak publicly on the subject. He hoped now to move on to other things and leave the problems of education to other people whom he had managed to enlighten. (Even Illich's own learning is not, apparently, as much under his own control as he might like.) Then he said: "I trust men constantly to use their hearts and their brains. I want to live in a transparent society in which each moment of life is surprising and with meaningful participation in mutual education. I want to live in mutual education up to the moment, and in the moment, of my death."

About the Contributors

ROY P. FAIRFIELD is a professor of social sciences at Antioch College and Coordinator of the Union Graduate School.

HERBERT GINTIS is an associate professor of education at Harvard University.

MAXINE GREENE is a professor of English and educational psychology at Teacher's College, Columbia University.

COLIN GREER is Executive Editor of *Social Policy* Magazine, Director of the University Without Walls at Staten Island Community College, and author of *The Great School Legend: A Revisionist Interpretation of American Public Education* (New York: Basic Books, 1972).

RONALD GROSS, a teacher and poet, is presently an adjunct assistant professor of social thought at New York University. His books include (with Beatrice Gross) *Radical School Reform* (New York: Simon & Schuster, 1970) and *The Arts and the Poor* (Washington, D.C.: U.S. Office of Education, 1969).

IVAN ILLICH, a cofounder of the Center for Intercultural Documentation, Cuernavaca, Mexico, is the author of *Deschooling Society* (New York: Harper & Row, 1971).

JUDSON JEROME is on leave from Antioch College and working on a book about contemporary commune movement. He is the author of *Culture Out of Anarchy* (New York: Herder & Herder, 1971).

ARTHUR PEARL, chairman, Committee on Education, University of California, at Santa Cruz, is the author of *The Atrocity of Education* (New York: New Critics Press, 1972).

NEIL POSTMAN, a professor of English education at New York University, is coauthor of *The Soft Revolution* (New York: Delacort, 1971).

SUMNER M. ROSEN is the Director of the Training Incentive Payments Program, Institute of Public Administration, New York City.